AFFLUENCE INTELLIGENCE

Earn More, Worry Less, and
Live a Happy and Balanced Life

Stephen Goldbart, PhD

and

Joan Indursky DiFuria, MFT

Da Capo
LIFE
LONG

A MEMBER OF THE PERSEUS BOOKS GROUP

Design and production by The Perseus Books Group

Cataloging-in-Publication data for this book is available from the Library of Congress.
First Da Capo Press edition 2011
ISBN: 978-0-7382-1424-5
e-book ISBN: 978-1-59315-693-0

Published by Da Capo Press
A Member of the Perseus Books Group
www.dacapopress.com

Da Capo Press books are available at special discounts for bulk purchases in the U.S. by corporations, institutions, and other organizations. For more information, please contact the Special Markets Department at the Perseus Books Group, 2300 Chestnut Street, Suite 200, Philadelphia, PA, 19103, or call (800) 810-4145, ext. 5000, or e-mail special.markets@perseusbooks.com.

CONTENTS

ACKNOWLEDGMENTS

We wish to thank the many colleagues and friends who have contributed to the evolution of this book. First and foremost we want to acknowledge Elsa Dixon, whose writing, editing, and wonderful ideas helped make this book happen. She is a gem. We also are indebted to Marc Gerald, our literary agent, who saw the book's potential and gave strong encouragement and steadfast support throughout the development of this project. We thank Katie McHugh, Executive Editor at Da Capo, for choosing this project, and whose editorial assistance and hard work moved the manuscript along.

We want to express our deep appreciation to all of our clients, from whom we have learned so much, and a special thanks to those who have allowed us to share their stories and their lives in this book. We thank you for your willingness to trust us in our work together; it has been our privilege and pleasure to be of guidance in helping you find the balance of wealth, health, and fulfillment. We also want to express our appreciation to our colleagues, particularly those who have been steadfast supporters of our work: Stacy Allred and Karen Klein with Merrill Lynch; Dick Trumpler of NY Private Bank; Idelesse Malave, former Executive Director of Tides Foundation; Peter White and Jay Hughes, Jr., who have been sources of inspiration and wisdom; Dennis Jaffe; Paul Schervish; Mark Roberts; Darcy Garner; John Staab; Mary Mewa; Terry

Ruddy; Robert Graham; Barb Culver; Dennis Pearne; and Megan McNealey-Graves—all who have contributed their encouragement and support of our work.

Each of us also wants to acknowledge our gratitude and appreciation to family and special friends:

I, Stephen Goldbart, would first like to thank my wife, Estelle Frankel. Without her continual support and encouragement my participation in this book project would have been virtually impossible. She has been my muse, and has provided invaluable advice. Throughout it all she has been a compassionate and loving partner. I would like to acknowledge the support of my son, Elan, who deeply understands the importance of living one's values and using Permaculture design for regenerative global solutions. A special thank you to my sister, Dr. Dorothy Clark, English professor and poet, who has also been a source of moral and intellectual support. And my parents, Mayer and Rachel Goldbart (may they rest in peace), who never failed to provide me with unconditional love, support, and encouragement. They were amazing models of courage, resilience, optimism, and fortitude. I would like to acknowledge the love and sustenance of my close friends and colleagues: Dr. Andrew Condey, psychologist/wilderness guide; Dr. Adam Duhan, physician and satirist; Rabbi Michael Lerner, who has always been a good friend and unstinting supporter, saw our potential in the early days, and was among the first to publish our work; Michael Ziegler, fellow BNO brother and passionate supporter. Like my family, they provided support when I was troubled and shared in the triumphs along the way. Their enthusiastic encouragement (and at times, blind optimism) was and always will be greatly appreciated. Finally, I want to thank all of my consultees and colleagues for their ongoing support of this project.

I, Joan Difuria, want to express my deepest gratitude and appreciation for the many important people in my life who have supported me both personally and professionally. First and foremost I want to acknowledge my sons Ross and Jay, who are my greatest gift in life, and whose love and support has given me an immeasurable amount of meaning and purpose, the importance of which I can only get from having them in my life. I also want to thank Robert Fisher, my life partner, for his keen business acumen and wisdom, and for his remarkable capacity to be patient, loving, and supportive. He is my greatest advocate, always offering endless enthusiasm for my work. I want to thank my siblings Alan, Lois, Ruth, and Barbara, who are my family but more importantly my friends and anchors, for being my cheering section. Chuck Gompertz, my dear friend and business mentor, for his enduring guidance, support, and generosity as a human being. To my father, Harry Indursky, who taught me so much about business, and about persistence and dedication. My mother, Evelyn, who taught me family first—you will always be with me. And of course, my friends, who are invaluable to me and who on a daily basis have lived through my trials and tribulations. You all enrich my life and encourage me every day, being at my side and loving me the way you do.

INTRODUCTION

This book will teach you about people who are financially successful and what they did to attain wealth, happiness, and fulfillment.

As the cofounders of the Money, Meaning & Choices Institute,
we are well acquainted with the issues of wealth and happiness. In
1999 we coined the phrase "Sudden Wealth Syndrome" to describe
the challenges and opportunities faced by people of new wealth,
and to our surprise, practically overnight we were overwhelmed by
attention from the media, being interviewed on radio and television, and in newspapers and magazines around the world. This was
the era when, according to the *San Francisco Chronicle*, the Bay
Area alone was minting sixty-four new millionaires a day. Yes, this
was a moment in American history of what today we might call
"radical hubris," and what others have called "irrational exuberance."

We got attention because we were telling a counterintuitive
story: Coming into money did not solve people's problems or make
them happy in an enduring way. In interviews with the media, we
were repeatedly confronted with sarcasm and disbelief on the one
hand, and real curiosity and excitement on the other.

Most people are convinced that if they have tons of money,
they'd be happy. While it is easy to assume that people who have
money are happy, the truth about their lives is far more compli-
cated than the size of their bank accounts. In general, the more
people make, the more they want—and the more they have, the

less joy it brings them. Dan Gilbert, a psychology professor at Harvard University and the author of *Stumbling on Happiness,* asserts that once you have enough money to meet your basic needs, a lot more money won't actually make you much happier. The reasons behind this are simple, but defy conventional wisdom. First, people tend to overestimate how much pleasure they will get from material objects—although, despite this, they continue to return to the mall or car dealership in search of more—a dynamic that economists call "the hedonic treadmill." Also, money tends to create problems of its own, such as increased stress.

Think of Howard Hughes, who died with a fortune, but paranoid and alone. Or the late Diana, Princess of Wales. She married into one of the wealthiest families in Europe, lived in a castle, and had any material thing she wanted, but by her own admission she was totally miserable. Then there are the people who have that special something, who enjoy a quality of life that we would all love to have. What makes them different from the rest of us is something we call *Affluence Intelligence,* and this book will show you how to get the peace, satisfaction, and happiness that they have.

The surprising truth is that we all reach a saturation point when it comes to money. Having $10 million does not give you more happiness than having, say, $8 million. In fact, a recent Princeton University study discovered that the numbers for happiness and money are far more modest. In fact, the researchers found that people were generally unhappy due to a lack of money up until about $75,000 a year. The lower a person's annual income fell below that benchmark, the unhappier he or she felt. But the more surprising thing researchers discovered was that no matter how much more than $75,000 people made, they didn't report any greater degree of happiness. This is due to something called the law of diminishing returns, where you put out more and more effort but at some point you start to get less and less back.

We spent almost two years as the focus of a media frenzy, perhaps because at the very heart of our work is the formula for the twenty-first-century version of the American Dream. While wealth creates problems for some, we have also had the privilege of being on the fascinating journey with those who achieved "the Dream"— who through ingenuity, optimism, timing, smarts, people skills, and sheer persistence obtained what most of us want: money *and* fulfillment. As we spent more time with the affluent, getting to know who they are and what makes them tick, we arrived at an astonishing discovery: They are made up of the same chemistry and capacities as the rest of us. They are you, and you can be them!

So here we are again telling a story that most people will not believe: true affluence can be obtained by anyone; all you need is the courage to honestly face your strengths and vulnerabilities, to be open to change, and to be willing to make use of the Affluence Intelligence strategies found in this book.

Our program is a way for you to become rich that not only brings together the best of your head, heart, and spirit, but also includes personal satisfaction and emotional connection. Is it about more than just money? You bet. Following this program will enable you to have more money, but it will also show you how financial success ultimately rides on something bigger than just your net worth.

We have written this book during a time of financial upheaval and when many institutions—banks and financial organizations— seem broken. In the wake of the Great Recession, many of us are thinking about how we can reinvent our lives, as well as questioning our expectations about money—how much we should spend, save, and share? What role should money have in our lives? How much should it shape our destiny? It is during times of crisis that windows of opportunity open but are often hard to see. There is no better time than now to rethink your relationship to success and fulfillment. By reading this book, you will come to understand what it takes to develop Affluence Intelligence, and see that attaining the affluence that others seem to have is within your power. You will learn, as we have learned from the lives of our clients, how money is an important aspect—but not the whole—of affluence. The personal work you do can change the direction of your life, bringing to light what truly matters to you. No one else can do it for you. Our unique three-month, step-by-step plan can help you get there.

Chances are that you intuitively understand that tapping into this intelligence is something that could help you. But how can you know for sure? It's a clear sign that you need to harness Affluence Intelligence if you feel any of the following:

- ❏ I feel that there is never enough.
- ❏ I've lost a sense of where I want to go.
- ❏ I don't have enough time to do what I like to do.
- ❏ There is never enough time to spend with loved ones.
- ❏ People want more from me than I can give them.
- ❏ I'm not living up to my potential.
- ❏ This is not supposed to be my life—what happened?
- ❏ No matter how hard I try, I just can't get where I want to be.
- ❏ What used to make me happy no longer makes me happy.
- ❏ I fear for the future.
- ❏ There's a disparity between how I spend my time and what I really want to do.
- ❏ Life is passing me by.
- ❏ I just don't feel satisfied. There has got to be something more.

If any of these statements resonate with you, then you will likely benefit from learning about Affluence Intelligence and finding out how you can increase your own.

Tackling psychological issues and challenges such as tapping into a new way of thinking can be daunting at the best of times.

And in the wake of a major recession, the stress of financial difficulty combined with the uncertainty of the future can send a person into a full-fledged crisis. At the Money, Meaning & Choices Institute we believe that a crisis is a time of rich opportunity for personal change, because we have seen it happen time and time again in the lives of our clients. Generally speaking, people don't usually shake things up when life is going comfortably as planned. Instead, it often takes real discomfort to motivate someone to make true change.

But in this book, we will help you make those changes in the easiest and most effective way possible. In Chapter 1, we will give you a better understanding of what Affluence Intelligence is and what it can do for you. Chapters 2 and 3 outline the lifestyle priorities you will be asked to investigate for yourself. We suggest you read each of these chapters carefully, even if you think that they don't pertain to you. (Resistance can be a powerful signal that, on an unconscious level, you are reacting to something that is actually essential to your development.)

In Chapters 4 and 5, you will learn about the key attitudes and behaviors of Affluence Intelligence and take a quiz to figure out where you stand. Armed with this new knowledge, in Chapters 6 and 7 you will learn about, and assess for yourself, the role of Financial Effectiveness. Granted, this is hard work, but it can transform your life.

Having come this far, you will now delve more deeply into the process and start to create real change for yourself. In Chapter 8, you will learn how to set the "thermostat" of your Affluence Intelligence, and how you may be getting in your own way. In Chapter 9, you will determine your total AIQ (Affluence Intelligence Quotient).

Then, toward the end of the book, you will start to put your new life plan into motion. In Chapter 10 you will create a plan to raise your AI thermostat to where you want it to be. In Chapter 11 you will follow strategies step-by-step for three months, thereby unlocking your Affluence Intelligence and starting to live, perhaps for the first time, according to your full potential. Finally, Chapter 12 will show you how your newly gained skills and mindset can transform your life.

Having Affluence Intelligence means having (and achieving) ambitious goals, living your priorities, and enjoying a greater sense of possibility. It also means enjoying the ride toward financial and personal success.

chapter one

MONEY, MEANING, AND CHOICES

*H*appy and successful people know something that their equally smart, well-educated, but poorer and discontented peers don't. Our client Brenda, a San Francisco attorney, put it bluntly: "I have a degree from an Ivy League college, and my husband and I work our butts off. We're smart people, and we're doing what we believe are all the right things, but we're always worried and struggling. It's even more frustrating when I look at Sally, my supervisor, who didn't go to a top school. She seems to start and end her day happy, has the time to go to daily yoga classes, takes six-week vacations, and makes way more than I do. Somehow she got the prize—and to top it all off she doesn't seem to have the continuing anxiety that Tom and I have."

For over a decade at the Money, Meaning & Choices Institute, we have used our senior-level expertise in business and psychology to help people to change their lives—and often those changes include having more money. We have worked to discover the secret ingredients of the twenty-first-century success story. We're sure you have puzzled over other people's rise to the top despite resumes and experience that are no better than yours, who may, in fact, have less education and who don't put in a 24/7 workweek. Despite appearances, they are doing something different from what you are doing. The good news is that you can learn to do it, too.

Prior to establishing the Institute, as psychologists we each worked in social services, private practice, and in the business world. Joan worked for a program that helped people with schizophrenia and manic depression; Stephen was a codirector of a public health program for severely disturbed adults. We have experience working with a wide range of people. On one end of the spectrum, we have helped with people in social services trying to find a job to support themselves, single parents who are struggling to make ends meet, hardworking and educated people who cannot seem to stay out of debt or break habits of underearning, and penniless drug addicts. On the other end are the CEOs of Fortune 500 companies, heirs to massive family fortunes, and the highest earners who simply cannot stop spending. In other words, we have worked with some of the richest and some of the poorest people in this country. As a result, we have developed an effective program to help people gain real financial *and* personal satisfaction and fulfillment. By unlocking your Affluence Intelligence, you will have the opportunity to reorganize and upgrade your life, to live a life more closely aligned with what is most important to you, and to make money your ally rather than your adversary.

Our unique understanding of affluence, and the program we built to help people get it, was born out of our direct experience with clients. Two, in particular, may give you insight into what makes some people thrive financially and achieve life satisfaction while others struggle.

David was an architect at a prestigious Bay Area firm. He was competent but not brilliant—we suspected he would never make senior partner at his firm, although he had a degree from an Ivy League school and earned an admirable salary. However, he and his wife, Ellie, had cultivated a sumptuous lifestyle that, now that she was no longer working, was just a little out of their reach. They were starting to get into debt. Ellie's father had always provided for her, and David knew he was expected by both his wife and himself to do the same. David had come to see us about his high level of anxiety, for which his doctor had recently prescribed Xanax. "I lie awake at night imagining that something's going to happen that will derail me financially," he told us. Not only anxious, David was adrift. He needed to change something—to find a new direction for both his work and his life.

Howard came from a very different background. He had dropped out of college to work at his father's business, a home appliance/electronics store. By the time he was thirty, Howard had expanded the business from one store into three and, by starring in a series of low-budget but popular TV ads, had become a local celebrity. Over the next decade Howard built a chain of popular stores and earned a high income that allowed him and his family to live in comfort—even luxury. Howard had come to see us because he wanted to make sure he provided for his children, but he did not want to spoil them or make them think they did not have to work to support themselves when they reached adulthood.

Having spent time working with both David and Howard, we realized that they had both been dealt similar hands. Both were ambitious, hardworking, and had the chance at a good education (although Howard had chosen not to see his through). Each earned an income that most people would envy. But while David was clearly unhappy and struggling, Howard appeared content. He was by no means a financial genius, but he had a belief in his vision and fire in his belly, and he was willing to take several big risks that had paid off very well financially. In contrast, David had achieved some big accomplishments (a degree from a good school, a job with a respected firm), but somehow, as he told us, "I feel that I have gotten stuck and am no longer enjoying my life." Being stuck meant he wasn't doing the kind of work that would lead to a promotion and a bigger salary, or at least that is what he feared.

What did Howard have that David didn't? We felt that the answer to this question held a precious secret just waiting to be discovered and shared. After we discussed the many people we had counseled over the years, we agreed that Howard (and others like him) had something that we decided to call Affluence Intelligence: that seemingly mysterious quality that made some people—often not the smartest, best educated, or most hardworking—able to create rich and fulfilling lives for themselves, to have money, and to be deeply satisfied.

THE ELEMENTS OF AFFLUENCE

To most people, the word "affluence" is synonymous with "wealth" and means having lots of money. However, affluence, as we define it and as our wealthy clients have demonstrated over and over again, includes the following seven elements:

1. Having enough money to meet not only your needs but also your desires.

Obviously, we all need enough money for the necessities—to eat, to have proper medical care, and to keep a roof over our heads— and it's relatively easy to calculate exactly how much money that is. But it's more difficult to calculate how much we need for non-necessities—the things that we desire and that would make us feel rich (or at least that we are living richly). Being affluent means being able to afford what you really want—whether it is a vacation home, a collection of vintage motorcycles, the freedom to take a sabbatical from work, visiting family abroad, or whatever else would thrill your heart.

Of course, how much we need for our desires varies greatly depending on what we want. One person might be dying for a Porsche 911. Another person might yearn instead for an experience, such as the ability to take off from work and hike in the mountains for a week. Each can be equally valid choices. When you think about what you want, the point is not to judge your desires as good or bad, but to determine how much money you need, not just to get by but to be affluent. Howard was not much of a spender, but he had the comforting knowledge that if he or his wife wanted something, he could probably afford to go ahead and buy it.

Those with Affluence Intelligence have found their unique financial balance point between needs and wants. There isn't a dollar amount that answers the question, How much is enough? (If I had $X million I'd be satisfied.) They use what they have to develop a financial strategy for saving, spending, and sharing, and the transferring of their money that is based on their core values, and is sustainable over the long term.

By unlocking your Affluence Intelligence, this book will help you determine your unique balance point, and what you need to do to reach it.

2. Doing work you like so much that you lose track of time.

Affluence means doing work you like so much that you'd do it even if you weren't being paid, because it engages and satisfies you on a very deep level. You may sometimes get so caught up in your work that you lose track of time and may have moments of great insight and creativity. Psychologists call this "flow." You don't have to be doing paid work to be in the flow. For example, volunteer work is something many affluent people find deeply satisfying. You might also be performing activities you enjoy such as gardening, dancing, or amateur race-car driving—anything that engages you deeply.

Many people have jobs that do not interest them, or that they find boring. Architecture had once been David's passion, but it no longer was—yet he had made no lifestyle changes to reflect his change of heart. Instead, he had fallen into a "gerbil on the wheel" existence, doing the same thing day after day in an effort to stay ahead. Living like this is not living in affluence. No matter how high your salary, you are not affluent until you spend time doing something that you truly love.

3. Having relationships that bring you joy.

Affluence means having relationships that work well and that make you happy and satisfied—whether at home or at work, and whether you have many relationships, or simply a few. Some people are introverts: spending time with others depletes their batteries, and they need lots of alone time to recharge. Other people are extroverts: being alone depletes them, and being with others recharges them. There is no right or wrong choice about how you spend your time, but it is important to be clear about what works best for *you*.

Affluence does not mean having as many relationships as possible, although it is great to be rich in friends. We're not talking about your friend count on Facebook (do you really need 700 friends?). Instead, we are talking about the people with whom you are really connected, who provide real comfort and satisfaction.

Some of our clients have an incredibly strong family bond, which they say is essential to their happiness and success. The Morrows are a four-generation ranching family that we see twice a year. In these multigeneration family meetings, family members take the opportunity to share very personal concerns, using the larger (more than twenty members) family group as a sounding board. There are always moments of joy and tears: a family member might ask for forgiveness for not having followed through with something they said they would do, or a college-bound young man may ask for feedback on his choice of a major. The Morrows have a priceless capacity to provide their family members with helpful and honest feedback.

Finding joy in relationships can be fraught with hardship, particularly when money becomes an issue. Finances were causing so much tension between David and his wife that they had started talking about divorce. This level of discord in a major relationship does not have a place in an affluent life. Although their income was in excess of $300,000 per year, they felt as if they were struggling to get by. While it is true that money issues are the number one problem in love relationships in the United States, those who have Affluence Intelligence know how to keep their money problems in perspective and out of the bedroom. The Beatles were right. Money doesn't buy love—or a life rich in closeness, emotional connection, or sexual satisfaction.

4. Being safe in body and mind.

Feeling comfortably safe and secure is a crucial element of having a rich life. Being affluent means achieving sufficient peace of mind so that you can sleep well at night and not be kept awake, anxiously worrying about what might happen in the future or ruminating regretfully about how you have dealt with money in the past. It also means being able to truly enjoy what you have, and not to feel guilty about money, or to feel you do not deserve what you have. David had another form of guilt, reflecting his own internal pressure. He felt he was not living up to his financial responsibilities, which included his perception of his wife's expectations, and was experiencing so much anxiety that he needed to use tranquilizers.

Being affluent also means having a sense of personal safety. It means living in a neighborhood where you do not feel physically threatened, and being able to afford physical protections—such as a safe car, a secure home, and comprehensive insurance in case of disaster—so that you can feel confident in your ability to protect and care for yourself and your loved ones.

5. Having power.

Those with Affluence Intelligence have personal power, and use it to attain their needs and wants. They come from all walks of life: people like Bill and Melinda Gates, Oprah Winfrey, or Warren Buffett. Their power is a product of their personal certainty, tenacity, clarity of vision, integrity, and money. They are conscious of how they exercise their power, and its impact, using care to foster positive and constructive outcomes for both themselves and others. Importantly, they respect the rights of others, and will not use power in service of "any means to an end."

In the United States, and other Western societies, money is power. This is not true in all cultures. In India, wisdom is power; in many traditional Jewish cultures, education is power. But in this country, when you have money, people listen to you. You control the purse strings, you call the shots. Having money puts you in a different place when it comes to having a sense of authority and influence in the world. However, having this kind of power does not necessarily mean that you have good self-esteem or are getting the love you want. And money is only power if you know how to harness that power and use it in the world.

Having power offers you a freedom of choice and a sense of autonomy and potency in the world. It puts you at the table when choices are being made; it gives you the opportunity to be in a position of being a decision maker and a leader. You have a say in the things that matter to you. A person who has power gains the recognition and respect of the community, whether that person is a corporate captain, a community organizer, teacher, or spiritual leader. By unlocking your Affluence Intelligence, you can have a significant impact and influence on matters that are important to you.

Howard, the electronics dealer who was a local celebrity, was recognized wherever he went in his hometown, and people were eager to hear what he had to say. The way he exercised his power was to offer leadership at local events that brought the community together for the underserved. Whether or not he chose to exercise his power, he took pleasure and security in just knowing that he had it.

6. *Living a life that has meaning and purpose.*

It may surprise you to learn that many wealthy people feel adrift in the world. This is a classic problem for people who inherit the family fortune. *Born Rich* is a 2003 documentary created by an heir to the Johnson & Johnson fortune about the experience of growing up in one of the world's richest families. It reveals the struggles of these young adults to define themselves, and to find purpose and motivation when everything they will ever need has already been provided.

Numerous studies have shown a worldwide three-generation phenomenon: Created wealth will be gone within three generations more than 80 percent of the time! Howard, for example, was concerned about the impact of the family wealth on his children and grandchildren—he did not want them to go adrift, with no sense of self or purpose.

But even people like David, who have earned their money, can feel that they are living fractured lives because they have become disconnected from what they know to be important and true.

You are not affluent if you are financially rich but feel, at the end of the day, that all the money you have amassed means nothing because some core part of your life is missing or has been forgotten. Instead, having Affluence Intelligence means knowing what is important to you, living in alignment with your core values, and having a sense of meaning and purpose. An indicator of what you value can be the amount of time you devote to those activities, people, or institutions that have meaning for you and give purpose to your life.

Time is its own kind of wealth. Managing your time effectively creates a rich and balanced life that goes far beyond simply making, saving, and spending money. More than just "having time," affluence means having a sense of agency, being in command of your time, and leading a life that is aligned with what you value most. How we spend our time in order to have a life rich in meaning and satisfaction changes as we age and as our core values evolve. In her twenties, Julie spent 80 percent of her free time in dance classes. She told us at that stage of her life, "I lived to dance." Her devotion to dance shifted when she was in her forties and was a mother of two young daughters, whom she adored and was passionate about parenting. She didn't stop loving dance, but now she gave it only 10 percent of her time.

Or consider Howard, the entrepreneur, who never works on Sundays. Sundays are time to spend with his wife and children— first they attend a church service, and then have a leisurely meal at their favorite local restaurant to share the events of the week.

David, on the other hand, was available whenever his Smartphone told him to be available. He was always apologizing for answering his cell during a family dinner or outing. He no longer loved the kind of work he was doing, and he was running so hard at life that he could hardly breathe, much less enjoy his work—or, for that matter, anything else.

7. Maximizing physical and emotional health.

Maximizing your physical and emotional health is an essential component of Affluence Intelligence. This means feeling good enough to function in your daily life without having disruptive or inhibiting physical or emotional symptoms. We often hear from our clients, "Health is everything." Maximizing your health requires working from your personal baseline, which varies with age, capacities, and any physical or health issues. If you have lost a limb or have HIV, you can still maximize your sense of physical and emotional well-being. Age is not always a limiting factor; there are some seventy-five year olds who feel better and are healthier than stressed-out forty year olds like David. Feeling healthy is a state of being that is fueled by an affluent state of mind. How people achieve their maximum varies with their priorities, passions, attitudes, and capacities. Those with Affluence Intelligence understand that emotional and physical health is a dynamic process that requires lifelong maintenance. Taking care of your mind and body, throughout your life, can allow you to remain healthy and becomes progressively more important as we contend with the prospect of illness and aging.

Once we had defined the seven elements of affluence we knew that it simply wasn't enough to be aware of these aspects of a fulfilled and happy life. So, we created a step-by-step plan that can help you turn your life around more quickly than you had perhaps imagined you could. While the journey to affluence can last months, years, or even a lifetime, it is remarkable what great strides you can make to overcome self-sabotaging habits in just three months, given the right guidance. From working closely with so many people over the years, we are convinced that everyone is capable of having Affluence Intelligence, although in most people it is lying dormant and is not being utilized. The potential to live a rich life is already there—we needed to help our clients like David to discover and capture it. We realized, then, that helping our clients unlock their Affluence Intelligence was the best way we could help them bring about powerful change in their lives—far more so than simply advising them on how to invest, suggesting career changes, telling them to moderate their spending, or any of the other advice traditionally offered by financial counselors.

THE AFFLUENCE INTELLIGENCE PROGRAM

We have discovered the four key areas necessary to unlock Affluence Intelligence:

- Priorities: These give direction and energy to your financial and lifestyle choices.
- Behaviors: These are the ways in which you act that foster or impede your progress in attaining Affluence Intelligence.
- Attitudes: These are the beliefs and mindset about money and your life, both conscious and unconscious.
- Financial effectiveness: The capacities of both *financial competency* and *financial ease* that enable you to be both capable and secure in your hands-on relationship with money.

Our program starts with an assessment of your strengths and vulnerabilities in these four areas—something that can be measured and quantified, just like your IQ. We call this score your AIQ (Affluence Intelligence Quotient), which shows you exactly where you stand, providing you with the information needed to increase your potential to become more affluent.

When it comes to affluence, we all have a baseline that we consider normal. This is based upon what you believe is true, your personality predispositions, and your social construction of reality. Your baseline is maintained in much the same way as your blood pressure and body temperature is maintained, by regulatory systems that are inside and outside of your direct awareness.

You can think of this method of regulation like a thermostat in your home. If your thermostat is set at 75 degrees and the outside temperature drops, the heater will automatically come on to warm up the room, or, if it gets too hot, the air conditioner will cool it down. The same is true of you.

Fortunately, like a thermostat, your AI quotient can be reset, and that's what you can do by following our step-by-step program to raise it, thereby unlocking Affluence Intelligence and starting to live, perhaps for the first time, according to your full potential.

HOW THE PROGRAM HELPED DAVID

David clearly needed to regain command of his life. His first step was to take the AIQ test, which measured his priorities, behaviors, attitudes, and financial effectiveness. David scored very low on the AIQ financial ease scale concerning his emotional relationship with money. While he was very comfortable with the mechanics of financial management, he was incredibly anxious about earning, saving, and spending money. His attitudes and behaviors were also mixed—in particular, he lacked initiative, assertiveness, and interpersonal effectiveness. His AIQ score was particularly low on having a sense of control in his life. But it was not all bad news.

In fact, David's strengths included great ambition, resilience, open-mindedness, and curiosity. While he'd always been a likeable and friendly guy who looked on the bright side of things, he hadn't realized these attributes could actually help him achieve affluence.

Examining his priorities was the biggest eye-opener for David. After careful thought, he realized that at this point in his life, wealth was not his priority. He was more interested in doing the things that brought him joy and peace of mind, and that made him feel useful in the world. But with his free-spending lifestyle, he was living as if having money were his priority. Having completed the test, David now knew his AI quotient—his strengths and vulnerabilities that were affecting his Affluence Intelligence.

THE MEETING

A few days after our initial conversation, we scheduled an all-day meeting with David at a hotel suite in San Francisco. We rarely agree to meet clients in an office venue—it's crucial to get them outside of a typical work zone to encourage freedom of thought and feeling. David showed up on time. He was a handsome, middle-aged man whose face was creased with worry and discontent, and he was dressed in expensive clothes that were somewhat carelessly put together. Everything about David suggested that he was an individual with great assets at his fingertips—European tailoring, and a very good barber—but somehow he lacked the ability or the motivation to add that final layer of personal polish.

As we settled in, Joan pulled out a large poster board and a Sharpie, and we got to work. One of our core techniques is to gradually paper the wall of the hotel suite with our client's own words. These quotes reflect our client's strengths and insights, as well as the areas of vulnerability that are holding them back. It is incredibly validating for clients to literally see that they have the answers to their own questions.

David's most important need was to reconnect his priorities with his daily life, and ultimately to rediscover the passion and creativity that had inspired him to pursue a career in architecture in the first place. He sat back in his chair, and started to tell us about the passion for design he had once felt.

"When I was a student, I was passionate about art and beauty. I could get lost for hours just sitting in front of a building whose lines inspired me. I'd walk around San Francisco in my spare time, looking out for the little design details that said something about the man or woman who'd designed them. I'd smile to myself every time I passed a certain bank with perfect Doric columns. It just made me happy." He paused, and shifted in his chair a little. "But then I fell in love with Ellie. She was amazing—so beautiful, funny, and confident. Suddenly all I could focus on was winning her, and proving that I could care for her as well as her very rich father had." He paused again. "I guess that's when things started to change."

David cared deeply about the environment, and had a dream of designing green, affordable houses for families. Instead, he was doing industrial design—competently, but without passion. What we have learned from working with clients is that affluent people almost always believe in what they are doing. Howard, with his low-budget TV ads, believed that he was offering top-notch goods and fine customer service, and he was. In contrast, David no longer believed in what he was doing, and this naturally (without him realizing it) had taken a toll on the quality of his work—and hence on his salary.

David was unhappy because he wasn't living according to his values, he wasn't unleashing his passion, and he wasn't using his unique strengths. Because of the lack of connection between his values, his true capacities, and his daily life, he was not making enough money to cover his lifestyle wants. Bottom line: because he felt there would never be enough, his anxiety about his finances was overwhelming him. But it wasn't enough just to tell him all of this. David had to connect the dots for himself, which he did after he took the AI quotient test. It allowed him to see in black and white what he held valuable and where his passions lay, instead of what other people wanted him to do and be. This in turn helped him to understand why he had become so unhappy.

David said, "I need to find the courage to either change what I do at work, or to get a new job."

Joan turned to David and asked, "How is it you were such a risk taker in college—technical mountain climbing, student body president, bungee jumping—and now it's hard for you to even imagine asking for what you want? Your AI quotient is low on optimism, initiative, assertiveness, and interpersonal effectiveness. This just doesn't make sense. Given what you've told us about your capacity to 'go for it' when you were younger, why is the gap in your capacities between then and now so great?"

We waited for David's response, as he sat silently, with his head lowered, lost in thought. He looked up and quietly began to say, "I remember myself as 'Mr. Just Do It!' but something changed when I had children." He lowered his head again, shaking it slightly back and forth. "I really believe that my role as a good father is to provide for my kids, keep my job secure, and not make waves. Asking for what I want seems selfish and could risk my capacity as a breadwinner."

Stephen asked, "Why can't you take care of your kids *and* yourself? Does being a 'good provider' have to exclude what really matters most to you?"

At that moment, David started to tear up. We felt the mood shift and the room sunk into a deep silence. Finally, David replied, "My mother passed away when she was about the same age I am now. I was only 11 years old—my family was shattered by her death. My father continued to go to work and provide for our physical needs, but he was just not there. His life seemed to be without joy, without satisfaction. He had never been a very high achiever, but he was always a nice, friendly guy, a person people trusted and felt comfortable with. Now he seemed like a man in chains. I remember him telling me, 'Well son, I'm so sorry about Mom, but that's life. We have to adjust and do what we need to do.'"

David looked up and said, "I can't imagine doing anything that would harm the stability of my home. Ever since I've had kids, I've been more and more afraid of dying, and the way for me to stay safe was to not move forward, or risk much of anything. So I've been sitting on my hands, stopping myself from living. Almost like my dad, I've done what I've needed to do to get by, taking as few risks as possible, without joy or creativity."

This was the pivotal moment in our work with David. We helped him see how he could use this new awareness to mobilize his capacity to take risks (within reason), unlock his Affluence Intelligence, and open the door to living that he had shut so many years ago. It was time for David to have work that he loved, and to take care of his and his family's needs for health, passion, and meaning.

The next step was for David to take everything he'd learned from our work together, and draft a new set of rules for his life. We call these Value Statements, and we use them to pinpoint exactly what is most important to the client at this moment in his or her life.

David wrote the following values statements:

I Value:
- Being creative in my work in order to express my passion.
- Exercising greater optimism at work and at home, to be more happy and successful.
- Taking initiative at work, and taking calculated risks in order to balance job security with job satisfaction.

- Making decisions that are aligned with my values so that I have a greater sense of control of my life.
- Having a more balanced lifestyle so that I can spend more time with my wife and children, and taking better care of myself.
- Making financial decisions to ensure quality of life.
- Living within our means in order to have a sense of security.
- Knowing the difference between needs and wants, to help control spending.
- Achieving a comfort zone with money, in order to reduce anxiety and pressure.

With clarity on his values and a desire to improve his AI quotient score, David was ready to put together his Affluence Intelligence Plan. First, he needed to set goals to bridge the gaps between how he was currently working and living, and how he wanted to be leading his life. David was a good, productive worker, but now, changing the kind of work he did over the following months became an essential goal to improve his AIQ. Another goal was to work with his wife to change their out-of-control spending. Luckily, as you will learn in our program, you can reset your priorities and then set new goals to reflect those new priorities at any time. David reset his priorities, and committed to developing assertiveness and initiative around what really mattered to him.

David now needed to take concrete *Action Steps* (the incremental changes and steps he would take to achieve his larger goals), and we helped him determine doable steps, using the framework of our three-month AI plan (as we will help you). He decided to write down and practice what he would say to his wife and his colleagues. David realized that he needed to take the next step and talk to both his wife and his partners to explain the new priorities in his life.

A week later, David scheduled a meeting with the senior partners at his architecture firm. It was the first time he had initiated a management meeting in over a year, which spoke volumes about how unhappy he had been. David looked at his three senior partners, and told them (remembering what we had told him about articulating needs and wants clearly and calmly), "I love working at this firm, but I need to be more creative. I have a proposal for you. Over the next twelve months I want to change the mix of my work. There is a certain type of project I really want to work on that is important to me. For the first six months, I would like to take 25 percent of my working time and devote it to environmentally friendly, beautiful, and affordable single-family prefab housing. Give me a year to see if I can make it profitable, and if I succeed I would like to discuss becoming a senior partner." They agreed without argument.

Later he sat down with his wife and said, "I love you, and I love our life together. But I need to live a life that reflects who I am. I want success to come from honoring, not ignoring, my real interests and passions. You know I've been so stressed and unhappy; but now I have a plan on how to be happier—with myself and with you and the kids. It starts with the need to make some changes in how we spend money. I think we could be happier with less, and I would like us to draw up a budget together to get us back on track." To his surprise, his wife was supportive of this new plan. She had been very concerned by how unhappy he seemed, and told him that material goods meant less to her than having David more present in her and their children's lives. She was very worried that David's stress level was eroding their marriage and believed that his new personal direction could improve it.

While the outcome of both conversations was successful, they had not been easy conversations for David. It required him to work on behavioral skills such as being assertive, and communicating clearly about his needs. He did this by practicing the exact words he was going to say until he gained a sense of comfort. He tried to anticipate what his partners might say so that he could be prepared with a response. But once he had stepped up and asserted his needs, he felt more confident about being able to do it again in the future. Also, with each conversation he took another step toward unlocking his Affluence Intelligence.

We told David to keep working the three-month AI plan by following the weekly action steps and to check in with us every month. This created accountability. (You can create accountability by finding an AI buddy, a friend, or colleague who will act as your coach in implementing your plan. We will explain in more detail how to do this in Chapter 10.) In the months that followed, David continued to stay aware of his old habits, such as not speaking up for himself, and to practice the behavioral changes he had decided to make as part of his action plan. As we do with all of our clients, we encouraged him to make changes that were sustainable. For example:

- David stopped staying late at the office and took more time to care for himself and his relationships. His values statements indicated he wanted to take more control of his life, have a more balanced lifestyle in order to spend more time with his wife and children, and to take better care of himself.
- He started exercising three times a week, occasionally taking his children on more weekend outings, and taking his wife out on a date once a week. Soon he did not have to take Xanax any more, his insomnia went away, and he was in much better health overall.

In addition, although money was not his primary goal, David saw a rapid rise in his "personal Dow," what we call the experience of becoming "financially effective" that comes with an increase in one's AIQ. Financial effectiveness is an empowering synergy of both self-worth and financial worth. It is more than just having more money; it is an increase in your overall Affluence Intelligence that results in feeling both in charge of, and at ease with, your finances and the chosen lifestyle that you have purchased. For David this meant focusing on projects with the kind of passion you need to make the quality of your work go from just okay to excellent. He had created his own brand of clean and green prefab houses (tapping into his love of the environment, beauty, and elegant design), and it had become very popular. Suddenly, he was making more money—although he was actually working less. But when he was working, he was more often in the flow. Needless to say, within that three-month period, David was very happy to finally have what he had always wanted—affluence.

We wanted you to hear David's story because we have seen, time and time again, how money follows Affluence Intelligence. When people focus on what is real and important for themselves, rather than only on the dollar sign, they can achieve "financial satisfaction," which is bigger than financial success. Yes, David had attained greater financial ease—he and his wife reduced spending, and created a budget that let them sleep easily at night. But what made it truly satisfying was the ways in which he had realigned his work and personal lifestyle with his deepest interests and passions.

A WORD ABOUT WOMEN AND AFFLUENCE

While the case studies we have used in this chapter are men, our program works equally well for women, if not better. Affluence, once almost exclusively the domain of men, is now increasingly being achieved by women. The number of wealthy women in this country is increasing yearly—whether by them owning their own companies, earning high salaries, or through marriage or inheritance. Claire Behar, the Director of New Business Development at Fleishman-Hillard, estimates that over the next decade, women will control two thirds of consumer wealth in this country, and be the beneficiaries of the largest transference of wealth in our country's history through inheritance from both parents and husband, estimated from $12 to $40 trillion.

However, women sometimes experience unique challenges when it comes to finances. No matter how they have accumulated their wealth, women's financial behavior and psychology are significantly different from men's when it comes to earning, spending, saving, and sharing money. As a general rule, women:

- Do not ask for as high a starting salary as men.
- Are more risk averse than men.
- Are more likely to give their power away or do not recognize that they have power.
- Believe they are lucky if they have money (whereas men usually believe they have earned it and/or deserve it).
- Are less likely to believe that they deserve a raise. And still earn less than men.
- Are less assertive in asking for what they want.

For these reasons, and because women typically live longer than men, the Affluence Intelligence program can bring about even more dramatic change in the lives of women.

WHY AFFLUENCE NOW?

We have just come through the worst recession many of us have seen in our lifetimes, and we are *all* feeling the pinch these days. Layoffs threaten, foreclosures loom, and credit card balances are sky-high. In times like these, it's tempting to think that simply having more money will solve all of our problems. So we look for a better job, or we stay at the same job but work extra hours, all the time trying to cut corners and save wherever we can. Instead, we need to approach our financial problems with fresh methods, including accepting the possibility that our way of thinking has more of an effect on our financial life than anything external such as the stock market.

Having more money makes things easier, we've always told ourselves. But is this really true? Maybe—and maybe not. The surprising truth—often difficult to accept by people who are struggling to keep their heads above water—is that for those without Affluence Intelligence, money can create as many problems as it solves. Why? Because when they go unexamined, our feelings and beliefs about money are so deeply rooted that they drive our behavior in ways we do not always recognize or understand—affecting our daily financial and lifestyle choices in negative ways.

We ask that you keep an open mind while reading this book and going through our process. Change will be required of you, and change is never easy. But harnessing your Affluence Intelligence could be the biggest and best change you make in your life to achieve happiness and security for both yourself and your loved ones. In other words, you have nothing to lose, and everything to gain. So let's get started.

chapter two

THE FIVE
LIFESTYLE PRIORITIES

*Y*our AI quotient is a combination of the priorities, behaviors, attitudes, and financial effectiveness that shape your relationship with money, and how they influence your attaining the seven factors of Affluence Intelligence. In the following chapters we will address each of these key components of AI, and you will have the opportunity to take the AIQ test, assess yourself, and create a plan to make the changes you desire.

In this chapter, we will explore the priorities that drive those who have and have not unlocked their Affluence Intelligence—what leads people to behave in certain ways and why they make the choices they do concerning their money and lifestyles, in both good times and bad. We call these crucial drivers the Five Ps:

PRIORITY ONE: PROSPERITY—
GENERATING AND HAVING ENOUGH MONEY

Prosperity means being financially satisfied. It means that you have achieved a level of satisfaction that allows you to live a life that fulfills who you are and reflects what is most important to you on a very deep level. We all yearn for a fulfilled life. This is an area where people with Affluence Intelligence have much to teach us. They believe that the world is a place where they can build wealth and feel great about doing it. They believe the world has all the necessary resources for them to become prosperous, and that there is plenty of money to go around.

We all yearn for abundance. But people with Affluence Intelligence usually do not make money only to put it in the bank. Their goal is to afford a lifestyle that brings them purpose and joy—whether it be running a company, leading a nonprofit foundation, or traveling, sailing, or snowboarding. Yes, they enjoy building wealth, but their focus is not on mathematics—How much money do I need to have? They do not say, I want to earn six figures. Instead they ask, How do I make money by doing what I am good at? How can I build wealth by doing what I find interesting, by using my skills and resources, while doing the things that I love to do? When people with Affluence Intelligence make prosperity their priority, they have married building wealth with building self-esteem, as this reflects what is most important to them. Prosperity is the offspring of this marriage. Looking at their lives, we see that many such people align what they love to do with that which drives them to make money. Others may not love what they do, but they love achieving a personally defined goal—such as building a successful business or being the best they can be at their chosen craft or profession. They have a vision of what they want and have a deep conviction that they will get it. They will do what they need to do, even if it means a great deal of hard work.

Howard, the appliance store entrepreneur, loved being a pillar of his community, being known as a businessperson of integrity who cared about others, and someone whom people could trust. Without a doubt, his successful creation of wealth was driven by how well he used his personal resources. In good times or bad, Howard would do his best being Howard: he knew that he was a people person who could connect with others and make them feel good. That is who he was, not an MBA whiz kid or a business visionary. It is true that prosperity was a top priority for Howard, and he put in many hours at his company. But he put even more hours into the Rotary Club, his church, tutoring kids at the local high school, and being a Little League coach. When Howard was in top form, he was like Bill Clinton working the crowd. Howard ended each week, whether his business was up or down, with a deep sense of satisfaction and personal worth. As he put it, "My business is not about selling appliances. It's about making people happy and satisfied about meeting their household needs. The greater the percentage of my customers who are satisfied and happy, the greater the success of my company." A businessman assessing Howard's company might say Howard is following a customer service model. In reality, the success of the company was due to Howard simply being Howard. The more Howard used his natural gifts, the richer he became, and the better he felt!

Those who have unlocked Affluence Intelligence are keenly aware of the dynamics of their own market, as well as of the broader marketplace. For example, an art teacher knows that his or her resources and opportunities for teaching professionals are more limited than those of a software design engineer. Social and economic factors come into play, both for good and for bad, when it comes to making money in your chosen field. People who have unlocked Affluence Intelligence understand this, and use it to their advantage. By seeing the world as having the resources they need, they are willing to look beyond their one area of expertise and explore how the cross-fertilization of markets can lead to success. For example, an art teacher might develop a computer-based teaching program for learning-disabled kids. Or a yoga teacher might develop an "awareness through movement" project for corporate employees. With Affluence Intelligence, prosperity may come from within your existing circle, or it may be created when you are building connections and using resources that you would not normally use. A dance teacher we knew created a DVD about movement and relaxation to help executives feel relaxed and centered prior to meetings focused on resolving differences and disputes. This product was a big hit in the middle management corporate world, a realm far away from the dance studios and stage performances of most dance professionals.

Those who have prosperity as a priority have a financial strategy for saving, spending, and sharing their money. They continually work their plan, keeping the long view in mind, not getting mired in the details of what is happening in the moment. Sylvia, a forty-two-year-old systems engineer, left her job to be an entrepreneur in the IT world. She wrote a business plan that was highly ambitious, detailed, and rigorous in design. She set clear benchmarks for success that included financial and personal goals for herself and the core team. Knowing they would be required to put in endless hours in the start-up phase, Sylvia wanted her team to know exactly how the plan would directly benefit them. Everyone understood the risk of failure, and understood the expectations for high performance and integrity. Sylvia made a commitment to raise money for the enterprise without dipping into personal or family assets. She also took very little for herself until the company achieved sufficient financial success that could be shared with all of her team. This level of rigor, clarity of purpose, and collaborative style were critically important to her success.

Those who have prosperity as a priority also understand that saving and spending money is not the end of the story. Many of our clients, made rich from the tech boom of the 1990s, have found that their sense of prosperity is enhanced by how much time and money they can give back to the world. Bill Gates is a grand example of this. On a smaller scale, there are groups like Social Venture Partners, a venture philanthropy group started in Seattle that forms partnerships with nongovernmental organizations (NGOs) to help them develop financial sustainability and bring in needed business skills and money. The partners are donors who each give a relatively small amount of their wealth ($6,000 per year) and a lot of time (in some instances, as much as a full-time job) to build prosperity for the nonprofit groups that they are supporting. These donors use the skills and wisdom they have gleaned from their years of working with start-ups. They have achieved prosperity, and they feel more affluent helping others do the same. Prosperity is still a high priority in their lives, but the focus has shifted from themselves to others.

In contrast, we have found that people without Affluence Intelligence often believe that the world is a place of scarcity, that there will never be enough, and that there is only so much to go around. (Whether we see the world as a place of abundance or a place of scarcity is often rooted in childhood experience. We'll talk more about this in the chapter on financial effectiveness.) This goes for time as well as money; they think, "If she's taking time for Spanish classes, she won't have enough time for me."

People without Affluence Intelligence commonly confuse their wants and needs, making it difficult to separate what is truly necessary from what is desired but not essential. Just because they want something, they think they actually *need* it, so they pull out the credit card. They feel pleasure, and they feel empowered. But those feelings don't last for long. Eventually they feel the anxiety caused by this spending in the wrong direction, taking them away from their core needs. It's no secret that credit card debt is out of control in this country. Anxiety and depression are at epidemic levels and we believe that the two are related.

As counselors, when we see our clients spending recklessly, we want to get them to turn off their psychological autopilot; we want to throw a bucket of cold water onto them and say, "Let's sit down and really look at your life. What is making you so hungry or dissatisfied that you need to spend money you don't have and create all that anxiety for yourself?" We want them to step back from their ordinary way of thinking to look at their lives in a new way—in the way they would if they had unlocked their Affluence Intelligence.

Martin's journey to prosperity started at the gambling tables in Las Vegas when he was a college student. Although he was broke and struggled to pay his rent, he was a brilliant mathematician who took his know-how to the casinos and quickly found a way to win (legally, of course). He wasn't greedy—he was not looking to win millions. Like many people with Affluence Intelligence, he knew that he deserved to have enough money to do the things that he wanted to do, namely, to finish school debt-free and make enough money to launch his own business. And that is exactly what he did. He not only won enough money to fund his college education, he built a nest egg to start a new business venture in investments.

Martin loved ideas and learning, and he loved winning, but more than anything else he loved numbers. He harnessed that love of numbers and was fully engaged in creating, learning, developing, and doing whatever it took to grow his new venture. He worked days, nights, and weekends to build up his business, because he loved it so much, and he was very successful.

Did he succeed because he wanted to make a lot of money? No. He wanted to come up with the perfect algorithm for investment strategies. Did he succeed out of sheer persistence? Perhaps. He told us, "To succeed, you have to be willing to walk through walls." His focus was clear, and his commitment firm, so nothing could get in his way.

In addition, Martin believed in having the best advisors possible to share their opinions and ideas. Martin was adept at listening closely and seriously weighing all viewpoints—and then, at the end of the day, making his own decisions.

In later life, Martin came to talk to us about his family, the wealth that he had amassed, and the family dynamics surrounding his money. Martin's priority was prosperity, but that was not his adult children's priority. They wanted him to do good in the world by giving even more money away than he already did. "After all," they asked, "what is the benefit of holding on to money when it can do so much to make a difference to other people?"

Martin wanted to keep working and accruing wealth, but his children were asking, "How much is enough? You have enough money to never have to work another day in your life. You can live off the yield and never touch the principal, so why do you want to make more money?" They wanted him to focus more on giving the money away and less on accumulating greater wealth. Martin understood what his children were asking, but it was unfathomable to him to stop working. He loved growing his wealth, but more importantly, he loved the opportunities that came with pursuit of wealth; it was part of his enjoyment in life. For Martin, building wealth and giving back to the community was a priority, as he was involved in several charities to which he gave a large sum of money every year (although his children felt he could give more).

Martin didn't want to stop working, but he did want to find a better balance in his life. (Of course, this is something we applauded.)

Martin wanted enough time to develop other interests, to own a vacation home in the place where he loved to surf, and to be able to help his children discover their own identities and life pathways. Also, since he had been divorced for many years, he wanted time to find a long-term relationship. We were able to help Martin achieve these goals and to create a life of true affluence that did not only mean having lots of money—it also involved some of the other factors that we will discuss in this chapter. Having prosperity as a priority, which also enabled him to live his passions, had made it possible for him to build such a rich life.

Those who have unlocked their Affluence Intelligence, like Martin and Howard, have something in common: When it comes to spending on lifestyle, they have always lived within their means. Warren Buffett is the quintessential example of this. Despite having $37 billion, Buffett still lives in the same five-bedroom house in an Omaha, Nebraska, suburb that he bought in 1958 for $31,500.

Others typically develop more expensive lifestyles as their portfolios grow, but they do not take risks that could "kill the goose that laid the golden egg." To outsiders, it may look like they are "living large," but in fact their lifestyle spending is a small percentage of their overall portfolio. When prosperity is a priority, those who have Affluence Intelligence may leverage money to make a business succeed (and they often take big risks with some of their own and other people's money), but they manage their debt very carefully. Yes, they do what they enjoy, but they know, to quote a client of ours, "A capital nest egg is very hard to build, and very easy to lose." Those who came from nothing are not willing to risk going back to nothing again.

Sadly, our society is rife with examples of those who have vast amounts of money but fail to live within their means. Surf the web, pick up a magazine, or listen to the news: there are professional athletes, celebrities, and lottery winners whose spending goes into the stratosphere once they've made or received a lot of money. We have seen that no matter how much money one has, even in the hundreds of millions, it is possible to confuse needs with wants, and to spend in a way that creates the same debt scenario of the typical American consumer.

PRIORITY TWO: PEOPLE—BEING WITH FRIENDS, FAMILY, COLLEAGUES, AND INFLUENTIAL PEOPLE

If people are a priority to you, you truly love fostering and furthering your relationships. People are a source of nourishment—and at times, rejuvenation. They are also a resource for creative personal and business collaborations. How much time you spend with others is a major influence on your behavior. We hear from women more than men that their support system comes primarily from their close friendships. Molly told us, "I don't know what I would do without my best friend. I tell her everything and she is the first person I go to when I have great news, sad news, and difficult times in my life. My friendships are priceless!" For Molly, her sense of fulfillment and personal satisfaction is closely tied to her connection with her friends and with her life partner. Many women put their careers aside—or give them up completely—to care for their children. While some women feel an obligation as well as a deep desire to stay home and take care of their families, others feel doing so is more of a sacrifice. The same may be true for those who are part of what is called the "sandwich generation"—they are caring for their children and elderly parents simultaneously. Those who are single parents may find that they are the only caregiver available.

Sometimes such women (or men, such as househusbands) feel badly about their choices, because they are not contributing to the household financially. But this kind of thinking does not take into account the amount of "sweat equity" being invested in the family. For many, taking care of home and family brings them a sense of meaning and purpose: it makes them feel rich and fulfilled. They are engaged in activities that enhance their self-esteem, provide love, and make a significant contribution to the essentials of successful family life.

Having people as a priority can catalyze a true sense of affluence in the world of work. Our client Ron came to us one day and said, "Teach me how to be rich." Ron was the only member of his family to leave their small rust-belt town that was, as he said, "on the wrong side of the tracks." He went on to earn an undergraduate degree in engineering and was employed in the technology world. Starting from nothing, Ron co-created a company that allowed him to walk away with hundreds of millions of dollars by the age of thirty-eight.

The formula for Ron's success was that he understood that being successful not only required his hard work but, more importantly, involved finding the right people to build the right team. Ron understood at his core that leveraging resources would expand opportunities and lead to success, and that human resources were the most important of all. Ron was a very analytic and strategic thinker; he would set a goal for himself and would come up with a plan to find the right people to help him achieve that goal. Most of all, he had a very positive attitude about other people. He liked them and would give them the benefit of the doubt. When people failed him, he would first try to ameliorate the situation, assuming that they had the best of intentions. If, however, they continued to fail him, he would let go and move on.

He told us, "I have learned that you must surround yourself with the brightest and the best, and that is what I have done. I have worked hard and made more money than I ever thought possible.

Now that I have sold my business, I want to succeed at keeping and growing my money. I want to build the best and brightest teams to help me with this task, and with whatever projects I choose to do."

His motto was "One plus one equals four." He believed that more than one brain was the best approach to business and to life. He made it a point to know everyone, from the little old lady who lived next door to a corporate higher-up who might open up new opportunities. He happily connected people with others, whether they were in business, on the basketball court, or in the neighborhood preservation group.

Like many other affluent people who come to see us, Ron wanted more balance in his life. He told us that his goal was to "be happy, and to create a family." Given what we had seen of his people skills, we had no doubt that he could make that happen. Soon after we gave him our "permission" to spend less time at work and to use his love of people on a purely social level, Ron soon met and married a wonderful woman. They now have two children.

Some people, such as Howard, are "people persons" and are naturally gifted at networking, bringing the right people together, finding and working with mentors, befriending people with authority, making clients feel valued, and so on. These people skills, this way of appreciating and enjoying other people in a genuine way, can help a person in his or her given career and can contribute to building wealth. Being a natural networker does more than simply create financial opportunities. When connections are made, you get a sense of personal fulfillment and empowerment. You have made something happen, or opened a door to something happening. When you're using your natural gifts, you feel that you are in the flow and doing things that reflect what is most relevant and personally gratifying for you.

With Affluence Intelligence, your engagement with people can leverage prosperity, if you have chosen a path that truly reflects your deeply held values and engages your core capacities.

Women and men can have varying reactions to hours spent with people. Many women complain that they do not have enough money, but they do not see that they are spending too much time and energy taking care of others, and that this behavior is getting in the way of their making money. They have not become aware of the impact of how they have chosen to spend their time. Or, if they do not have to work because they are financially stable, they might say, "I have so many people I need to spend time with, I never have enough time for myself." Our client Celia, for example, realized that she needed to spend less time having lunch with friends, because she would have preferred to spend some of that time on something that was perhaps more meaningful to her, such as learning to play the piano.

When it comes to spending time with people, men tend to have the opposite problem. (We are not trying to propagate gender stereotypes here, but during our years at the Money, Meaning & Choices Institute we have found this to be true.) Men are much more prone to spending twenty or thirty years developing their careers and then discover that their children do not know them. We have heard quite a few men say, "Gee, I wish I had spent more time with my kids. It's too late now."

If people are truly your priority, there is no single answer to how much of your time should be spent in relationships. But we do advocate achieving a balance in terms of how much time you spend with people, balancing love, commitment, and obligation. Of course, the nature of this priority will vary (as is true with the other priorities) according to your stage of life. There is no good or bad here—just the need to be sure, if you are seeking to unlock your

Affluence Intelligence, that you are making conscious choices about whom you choose to spend your time with and how you spend that time.

PRIORITY THREE: PRODUCTIVITY— ENGAGING IN ACTIVITIES THAT ACTIVELY MOVE YOU FORWARD IN YOUR LIFE JOURNEY

We think of productivity in two ways: (1) Productivity (work): doing the activities that earn you a living; and (2) Productivity (other): doing the activities outside your employment that may or may not earn you money.

With Affluence Intelligence, when productivity is a priority you are consciously and unambivalently engaged in your life. You are connected to what you're doing, getting things done, and moving yourself forward. Without having clarity of intention and of action you can be very busy and doing lots of things, but those things may not actively move you forward in your journey or engage you in your life. In fact, engaging in multiple activities may create a false sense of being productive, which may keep you from doing what you really want and need to do in order to achieve affluence. A woman dashing around town with an armload of dry cleaning and a batch of cookies for the PTA meeting might appear to be productive, but if her dream is to become a sculptor, these tasks and chores (which could be done by someone else) may actually be getting in the way of her achieving her true goals.

Keep in mind that productivity doesn't have to look busy. For example, a monk who is meditating is actively moving himself forward in his journey to enlightenment even if it appears from the outside that he is doing nothing. Intention is a key factor in productivity. For example, the same action (such as gardening) can be productive for one person and not for another. Claudia loves to garden. It feeds her soul and relaxes her, and then as a result she is more productive in her job as a director of human resources. Brenda, on the other hand, hates to garden, but she keeps a small garden on the balcony of her condo because her mother believes all homes should have plants, and complained until Brenda got some. For Brenda, caring for the plants is just one more item on her to-do list.

Sometimes, when we talk to people about productivity, they get defensive. They say, "Well, if I had all the money in the world, I wouldn't have to work so much, and then I would have more time to do the things that I really want to do instead of all the things I have to do. Then I could do *x*, *y*, and *z*." But what we have learned from decades of experience as professionals is that our clients will show up for their appointments, no matter how busy they are. They *make* the time if they feel it is important to actively move them forward in their journey. The key words here are *actively moving them forward in doing what is important to them in their lives.* If you want to be more productive, you must be productive and conscious about how you move toward those goals.

In today's world, with so much competing for your attention, it is easy to feel that you are accomplishing a lot when you actually are not. Many people spend a lot of time handling administrative tasks such as bookkeeping or answering unnecessary e-mails, but then they complain that they don't have the time to do the things that bring them joy. Often, having no time to do the things we *want* to do is a false story we tell ourselves.

We live in the real world, and we understand that many of us have obligations every day such as going to the supermarket, doing the laundry, taking kids to soccer practice, fixing the garage door, and so on. These things simply must be done. We would not suggest neglecting these obligations, but rather to see if there are other ways to fulfill them (such as outsourcing) that may free up your time to engage in other activities that bring you closer to your goals. For some, these tasks may seem to detract from achieving productivity. For others, they are steps on the way to living a productive life. One of our wealthy clients truly values everyday tasks (such as the family laundry) because she feels it moves her forward on her self-defined life journey of meeting her family's needs.

The key is being aware that what *feels* like productivity may or may not actually be moving you forward. Take the time to seriously reflect on whether your choices are spinning your wheels or actively moving you forward toward your goals.

Interestingly, many of our very wealthy clients resist when we encourage them to hire a personal assistant in order to free up some of their time. They can easily afford to pay someone to do all the things that most of us complain about having to do. Instead they feel guilty, or they feel things won't be done properly. People get into the habit of thinking these miscellaneous chores have to be done in a certain way or they are not done right. Perhaps it's true that they won't be done as efficiently by someone else, but if you let go of that perfectionism over mundane tasks, what could you accomplish in the time you save? If we work with focus on those areas that bring satisfaction, even a half hour a day can make a remarkable difference in moving us toward where we want to go.

Productivity is not only important for creating wealth, but for other areas of life as well. Dennis is a very nice looking, physically fit, and responsible young man. At the age of thirty he was working his way up in the world of finance, earning a decent living, had good friends, and no problems meeting women and dating. Dennis had a job as a financial analyst for a midlevel company—not a prestigious job, or one that would ever make him rich, but one that he was good at and enjoyed. When he got up in the morning, he knew what he was going to do for the day. He was happy.

Dennis occasionally bought lottery tickets, although like most people he never expected to win. One day, he hit the jackpot. Now he gets a $1 million check at the beginning of every year, and will do so for the next eighteen years of his life. His only complaint was that he didn't know enough to check the box that would have given him the full $18 million up front. He told us, "I never won the lottery before, so I didn't know to check the box!"

When Dennis came to see us, we asked him what we ask most of our clients: "What made you call us?" He sat quietly with his eyes cast downward, seeming almost ashamed. Then he said, "I used to jump out of bed every morning, ready for my day. Now that I have all this money, I find it hard to get out of bed, because I don't know what I am going to do for the day. I feel lost.

"The only thing I want to do now is to leave the country," he continued. "That way I don't have to deal with the nagging discontent of not having a purpose in life." It was an embarrassing, if not humiliating, surprise to Dennis to suddenly find himself so adrift despite his instant wealth. He couldn't sleep and spent many anxious nights struggling with what to do and trying to understand why he was no longer happy.

Dennis had lost his sense of productivity, and yet he felt he needed to be better than ever before. "Winning the lottery is a sign that I am being called upon to do something as large as the size of my winnings. I need to make sure that I do something special with this money, and make a difference in the world." Anything less would constitute failure. Consequently, he felt so much pressure to do "the right thing" that he did nothing.

"What makes you happy?" we asked.

Dennis replied, "I am happiest when I go to Argentina and other third world countries and teach young children who would not otherwise get an education. I like to stay for a few months at a time. My anxiety goes away and I really enjoy myself. I love these kids; they are so appreciative, but I think they are doing more for me than I can possibly do for them. I feel uncomfortable as soon as I get on the plane to come back."

As we worked with Dennis, he discovered that at the heart of his interest was helping kids learn the skills in life that would allow them to have greater choices and opportunities in the future. When he was teaching kids, he was working again and achieving a goal. He was being productive—in other words, living his priority. Our work was to help Dennis achieve productivity without his having to go halfway around the world to do it, refinding his sense of life purpose.

With our encouragement, Dennis decided to make a difference in his local community. He started spending the majority of his time working with underserved children and teenagers at a local school, and coaching sports teams. Surprising himself, soon he didn't feel the need to go back to Argentina because, as he told us, "I didn't want to go. I needed to stay and work with these kids here who were depending on me so much. I was actually making a difference in their lives, and I was starting to feel happy again."

Like many of our clients who suffer from Sudden Wealth Syndrome, the impact of an abrupt major life change due to coming into money meant that Dennis felt he had lost his identity and sense of life purpose. Simply put, he didn't know who he was any more and didn't know what direction to take in life. And having a strong sense of identity is a very crucial part of unlocking Affluence Intelligence. Ironically, Dennis lost his Affluence Intelligence by winning the lottery, and had to regain it by reestablishing the productivity that he had had before—albeit in a different venue.

PRIORITY FOUR: PASSION—BRINGING
EXCITEMENT AND JOY TO YOUR LIFE

"What makes you happy?" is one of the most simple and yet most important questions we ask our clients. We're actually asking about far more than simply what makes them happy; we're trying to help them discover their passions.

Passion is a feeling in the body, not in the head. You can enjoy a lot of things, and doing them can bring you satisfaction, but when something is truly your passion, when you engage in that activity, you experience a change in your physical state of being. Further, you may feel passionate about art or playing the classical violin, but your passion doesn't have to be something elevated and erudite. You can feel passionate about playing soccer, knitting sweaters, or building model airplanes.

When passion is a priority, it pushes you into action. How do you know when you are really passionate versus when you simply enjoy something? You feel that undeniable force that propels you to achieve something in your chosen activity or interest. When you are engaged in it you are in the flow, and there is no question, no doubt that you are doing what you love to do. You are focused solely on that activity so that everything else falls away, time passes without you noticing it, any other obligations and concerns you may have faded into the background.

Amy, an energetic, smart, and articulate woman, lives according to her passions. When she was twenty-one, she married an up-and-coming entrepreneur who was more than fifteen years her senior. While also taking care of their four young children, she dove headlong into her husband's world of business. Her excitement and energy was unharnessed as she discovered her passion for being an entrepreneur, and she started her own business. Additionally, she loved meeting people who were stimulating and had power, whether they were politicians, business people, spiritual leaders, or artists. Most importantly to Amy, they were thought leaders. Her desire to be engaged and involved in this new world became all encompassing.

She told us, "I love to be around thought leaders, to participate where the action is. I love intellectual stimulation, and I love the access I now have to not only my community, but to the whole world! I feel such passion about the things I love to do, whether it is meeting important authors, politicians, writers or traveling around the world, or building my companies."

With Amy's involvement, her husband's business grew, and they amassed a small fortune. Her world and her involvement in her husband's business came to a crashing and crushing halt when she found herself at divorce court. Amy, in her thirst for life and her capacity to be optimistic, was unaware of the slow but steady unraveling of her marriage. However, like many people with Affluence Intelligence, Amy had the capacity to face the truth of the situation, acknowledge her mistakes, and move on.

Because of a prenuptial agreement, Amy did not walk away from the marriage with a lot of money. She decided she wanted to start a business of her own now that her children were old enough to not need her full-time attention. Even during the divorce, she never lost sight of her goal, which was to get involved in the world of art investment and real estate development as quickly as possible, so she immediately sold whatever she could in order to get the funding to start her own business. She was willing to do anything and everything to make it happen, and, like many affluent people, she was willing to work very hard. Amy began buying dilapidated foreclosed houses, fixing them up, and turning them into rentals. Her rental business grew in leaps and bounds, and eventually provided her with the level of wealth and comfort she had enjoyed during her marriage. This in turn allowed her to once again devote her time away from work to other activities she loved, such as hatha yoga. Amy was once again happy. She had stabilized her finances through her success in her businesses, which gave her the opportunity to build her art business and reengage with thought leaders from different industries. When passion is in the driver's seat of Affluence Intelligence, like it was for Amy, you feel joyful and fulfilled as your life is led by passion-filled activities.

People who have not unlocked Affluence Intelligence fall into two categories: The first is the group who are endlessly frustrated by the lack of passion in their lives, and those who have found that their passions lead to trouble. The first group are people with "passion frustration," in which their experience of passion is more in their heads then their bodies. Or their psychological issues interfere with their experiencing the pleasure of passion, resulting in their feeling guilty, or angrily frustrated, or depressed. They may see passion as a top priority, but somehow their daily lives do not allow them sufficient expression of their needs. They may find themselves lamenting the inadequacy of their everyday reality, that in their ideal life they could live their true, passionate self, but in this life they cannot.

The second category includes people who find that when their lives are driven by their passions (what one might call "destructive passions"), the result is hurt and disappointment, which undermines their self-esteem. These are people whose passions are unconsciously married to painful, unresolved emotional experiences. More often than not, they end up engaging in activities or actions that are undermining, such as drinking, affairs, gambling, or impulsive decision making, enacting and acting out the drama and trauma of their unresolved emotional baggage. So for the sake of their psychic survival, they attempt to bury these troubled passions in the unconscious to protect themselves from repeated failure and unhappiness. Unfortunately, this attempt is rarely successful, requiring the need for professional help to unlock these destructive patterns.

We all have a gap between the reality of our lives and the ideal that we wish we could live. How we manage that gap can make or break our success or happiness. What we have learned from our very successful clients is that they acknowledge what is missing, get over the disappointment, and then construct the best possible reality from their given circumstances. Or they develop a plan to build a new reality. Some of our clients have learned to contain or constrain the repetition of a passion that they have come to understand is due to frustration, repetition, or unresolved pain. For example, let's look at John, a man who is wildly attracted to unavailable women (a destructive passion) because his mother never consistently provided for his emotional needs. John learned that the repetition of being in relationships with unavailable women and not getting what he deeply wanted could be changed by focusing on passions that made him feel happy (such as finding available women). This change of focus, new experiences, and understanding of his past enhanced rather than diminished his self-esteem. As an adult, you have choices. You don't have to do what you've done before. Life is short, so get on with it! Those with Affluence Intelligence actively seek the passions that bring them joy and satisfaction, and when these passions take them on a detour, they take charge and build a new road to get where they want to go.

PRIORITY FIVE: PEACE—GAINING A SENSE OF CONTENTMENT, SATISFACTION, AND EQUANIMITY

When we think of gaining peace we usually think of doing quiet things: meditation, yoga, being alone in nature, tending a garden, listening to classical music, and so on. And these activities certainly can bring you a sense of peace. But you can find peace in louder and more active endeavors, too, like marching in an anti-war rally or campaigning for human rights. Even a game of beach volleyball can bring you peace, if it makes you feel contented and satisfied.

As a general rule, when peace is your priority, money may not appear to be the central driver of your actions. If you want more peace in your life—say, by learning to write poetry or by spending more time in church—you may be concerned about its effect on your financial bottom line. However, people with Affluence Intelligence know that peace and money are not mutually exclusive. In fact, they recognize that they need money in order to be able to do the things they want to do that bring them peace. As with so many issues concerning true affluence, it's often simply a matter of balance.

From the outside, Charlene looked like she had a charmed life. She came from a well-known family that had made its fortune in the oil industry, and she knew from an early age that she would inherit enough to never have to work a day in her life.

But behind closed doors, things were bleak. As a child, she was emotionally, physically, and sexually abused by both outsiders and members of her own family. Her mother and father repeatedly told her, "You're fat, stupid, and ugly." And she believed them.

Not only did she face this constant humiliation at home, she also faced it when she went out into the world, primarily because she was very overweight. "I will always remember how humiliated I felt when I went shopping to buy a car," she told us. "The Mercedes dealer asked me to sit in an area away from public eye because I did not fit the 'Mercedes image.' He also asked me to have the cab pick me up at the corner, not in front of the showroom."

By the time she was forty, Charlene's obesity and depression were so severe that she contemplated suicide. She decided to undergo bariatric surgery for her obesity, and also began psychotherapy. In her long journey of physical and emotional healing Charlene discovered her most important strength—courage. She had the courage to not only get over the terrible wrongs of her upbringing, but also to make new life choices.

Over time, during our work with her, Charlene created a new view of herself that reflected her true assets: her innate sense of gratitude, her close friendships, and her desire to give back to others who had less money, time, and love than she did. Charlene trained to become a counselor who worked with children from emotionally challenged backgrounds. She also created a foundation to fund specific projects related to obesity. Through these activities she finally found what she had never had before—peace.

Having money gave Charlene the resources to get the physical and mental health help that she needed. But she felt it was dirty money, because it came from people who called her ugly, stupid, and fat. The peace that Charlene has brought into her own life is worth a million times more. If you met her today, you would see a very different person than she was at the start of her journey. Today she is a woman who laughs, who feels a sense of her own power, who speaks with certainty but can take in ideas from others, and who doesn't apologize for her foibles. Although she has numerous physical problems that often leave her hospitalized, you would never know it to look at her.

As with many of our clients, as Charlene gained peace, she also discovered her comfort zone with money—something we call "financial ease." With a stronger sense of self and greater clarity, she was better able to grasp her finances, and learn to oversee them, in ways that brought her peace. When people gain peace and financial effectiveness, money anxieties are lessened, and they are better able to take charge of their financial direction. We have seen people who made peace a priority reach clarity about who they are, and become so comfortable with what they want, that they better managed their spending and their earnings went up! With Affluence Intelligence you drive money, money doesn't drive you. So listen to, and respect, the voice deep within you that desires peace and equanimity. Don't be surprised when money becomes your friend as you live a life in which you enjoy the benefits of unlocking Affluence Intelligence.

KNOWING AND LIVING YOUR PRIORITIES

Perhaps the greatest single difference between people who have unlocked their Affluence Intelligence and those who have not is that the former are living a life in alignment with their priorities. They are not doing what their parents or spouses or children want them to do, or that society wants them to do—they are doing what *they* want to do, because it's their priority, being fully accountable to the lives they have chosen but not having their lives overly defined by guilt, others' expectations, or past scripts.

Perhaps, for example, one such person is a woodworker. If doing that craft means deep fulfillment and getting to spend time with the people he loves, it does not matter that he does not make a lot of money, because prosperity is not his top priority. Or take a young woman who wants to move up in the business world. Prosperity is all she desires, and she is willing to sacrifice other things in her life, such as spending time with friends. For others, finding balance among the priorities is their goal. All of these are valid choices; it's just a matter of making *conscious choices*. We are talking about being very aware of how the choices you make reflect whether or not you are living your priorities, and what the payoff is for those choices.

These life choices are made on both a small and large scale. On a small scale, you might ask, Do I want to drive myself to the airport, or do I want someone else to do it for me? On a large scale, you might ask, Have I chosen a career that reflects what I really want to do with my life? We say: maximize your opportunities by making conscious decisions and then, once you have made those decisions, either enjoy the choices you have made, or change them. With Affluence Intelligence you can see how many life choices are not cast in stone.

It's important to realize that needs can change over time, and vary with age. If a man has spent twenty years building a business, and has neglected his family, he cannot be surprised if they do not feel a close bond with him. In general, young people are not as aware of what they are giving up to pursue goals as are older people, who may have a heightened sense of mortality. Generally, as you get older you become more attached to other people, and less focused on the dollar.

Of course, either is a legitimate priority at any age. The twenty-year-old Silicon Valley entrepreneur may be willing to work sixteen hours a day and not have intimacy and relationships, and this is fine, if it makes him happy. He is in the flow of the second Affluence Factor: Doing work you like so much you lose track of time. Even if his business does not succeed, he has made a valid choice because he is engaged in life in a way that is meaningful to him. When he gets to be forty or fifty, however, his priority may shift to peace or people.

For most of us, priorities are an unfolding, developmental process. They are evolved and refined throughout adulthood. The essential point is that you should be doing what you are doing because it is at the core of the life values you have today, not just because it's what you were doing yesterday. This means recognizing when a value you had in the past is no longer relevant, or needs to be radically modified. Stop for a moment and think: What are your core values today? Are these values aligned with your current life priorities?

Now you'll take the first part of the Affluence Intelligence Quotient Test, helping you to identify what your priorities are—and they may well be different from what you think that they are—and putting them in rank order.

TAKING PART A, THE LIFESTYLES PRIORITIES QUIZ

Assess your priorities, based on an average week of current activities you engage in today and what you would like the priorities to be one year from today. Looking at today and one year from now, place the priorities in order of importance (a rank order) with 1 as the highest and 6 as the lowest on the chart on page 71. (Just because you rank something as a 6 does not mean it is not important to you—it is simply not the *most* important.) This procedure will identify the gap between today's reality and what you would like to see change in the next year.

BEING HONEST WITH YOURSELF

One of the challenges of doing this kind of assessment is looking at yourself with an objective eye, because what we think is true about ourselves and what is actually true may well be two different things. For example, a man might be a good manager at work and say that people are a priority for him, and claim that he wants more quality time with his loved ones, yet if he only spends a couple of hours a week with his children, he is either not being honest with himself, or he is not self-aware. It can be helpful to get input on your answers from another person who knows you well, or to have them fill in the chart for you after you have done so, and then use the average of the two scores.

Determining your priorities requires a thoughtful mix of what is most important to you and how you spend your time. In some instances, time can be a powerful way to measure the extent to which something is a priority for you. If you spend hours every weekend perfecting your golf swing, for instance, that's a clear sign that playing golf is most likely a priority for you. Our client Lisa was working as a writer and was also in graduate school. A lot of the other students would tell her, "I wish I had time to write." But then they would say, "Hey, did you see *CSI Miami* last night?" If these students had used their time to write instead of watch TV, they would have put their time where their wishes were. For these students, peace (in the form of relaxation and leisure) took priority over productivity (other). There is no judgment here—completing the chart will help you become aware of how you're living your life. In our values retreat with our clients, which is a six-hour meeting in a quiet setting away from the office, we ask participants to do a snapshot assessment of how they are spending their waking hours in the domains of self, relationship, work, and community. We ask them to divide their time among these four domains on a percentage basis. For example, a person may spend 10 percent of time for self, 30 percent on relationships, 55 percent on work, and 5 percent on community activities (for example, volunteer) in an average week. It is always an eye-opener to see how you are really using the one commodity that money cannot buy—time. For that reason, it can be very helpful to sit down with pen and paper and make a list of how much time you spend on any given activity (working, spending time with family and friends, playing sports, pursuing artistic goals, spending time in church, and so on).

Looking at how you spend your time isn't the only way to discover your priorities. For example, Candace was a single working mother for whom passion was a priority (and that passion was playing the piano), but she could only sneak in an hour of practice twice a week when her kids were out on a play date. Just because she had to work—at least forty hours a week—as well as maintain a household did not mean that productivity (work) was truly her number one priority. For some people, having a daily yoga or meditation practice, or gardening, which may only take one hour or less per day, could mean that peace is a top priority. Remember that Affluence Intelligence includes elements such as "living a life that has meaning and purpose" and "enjoying good health." For some of us, these elements are a top priority, but in fact take relatively little time in comparison to spending time at work, being a parent, or taking care of the business of daily life. So looking at how we spend our time shows us the ways in which we use our life energy, but does not necessarily show what matters most to us, or what we do that makes us feel most alive and abundant.

So think carefully about how you spend your time, both in activities that you enjoy and those that you feel you must do to survive or fulfill responsibilities. Then consider, and make a leap, to what you could or would do if you could reduce those activities that you believe get in your way.

We know how hard it is to see oneself objectively. Even very wealthy people fall into the trap of not seeing their behaviors clearly. We had a client who was bemoaning the fact that she did not have the time to do the things she really wanted to do (like go to an exercise class, or have lunch with her friends) because she had to work. But the fact was that Sara's husband made close to half a million dollars a year. She did not actually have to work, but was under the influence of a deeply held belief that productivity (work) *should* be her priority. Indeed: she grew up in a family in which the work ethic was the number one, two, and three top values. She felt that if she didn't work she was "a lazy, noncontributing person." Sara's belief, formed in her family of origin, that she needed to work sixty-plus hours per week in order to be productive led her to tell herself a false story and prevented her from developing a broader, more relevant definition of productivity. We have clients with Affluence Intelligence who say, "If I work seventy hours per week and I want to exercise, then I will find the time to exercise." They will sacrifice sleep, dinners with friends, or whatever it takes to make the time to do what they deem to be important.

Sometimes a client will say, "I am really into peace; that is a priority to me." So we say, "Great! What do you do to bring peace into your life?" When they are not able to tell us, we know that there is a gap between what they wish were true and what is actually true. Because it is easy to say what is important without evidence, be sure to come up with concrete examples of how you spend your time with a particular priority.

In completing this chart, it is important to be honest with yourself. This means you must look at what you are actually doing in your current life, not a wish or fantasy about what you could be doing. Keep in mind that we always want to see ourselves in the best possible light, which may artificially merge the real and ideal about who you are and what you do. Please work at keeping the real and the ideal separate, and not fall into the traps of magical thinking or "I should have, could have, would have." For example, a man may want to be a good provider to his family, and may comfort himself with the thought that he is that good provider, whereas the truth is that he is an under-earner who has not focused on making money (and he could be making far more, given his education and training). Instead, he is focused on his passion—sailing. He may list prosperity as his number one current life priority on the quiz, but again, this would not be born out in his actions.

Here's another challenge to keep in mind: You are assessing what your priorities are today, not what they were ten years ago or what they were when you were in college. Our priorities naturally change over time. For example, an idealistic college student might want to change the world, so she joins the Peace Corps and goes to Africa to help build wells for clean water, where her hard work makes a difference in many villages. Her first priority is peace; productivity (other) is number two. When she hits twenty-five, however, she begins to think that maybe she alone cannot heal the world, and that she should turn her focus onto herself and her own life. She returns to the United States and develops her career as an events planner. She starts to make money, which she still uses to help families in Africa, but her focus has shifted. She still works very hard, and productivity (other) is still a priority, but prosperity is now number two and peace has dropped to three. This is a normal developmental process—our values and life goals evolve as we learn and grow throughout adulthood. Taking the Affluence Intelligence quiz is a measure of who you are today, and who you want to be one year from today.

A WORD ABOUT PRODUCTIVITY (WORK)

The most common feedback we get on this test is: "Well, it's all right for wealthy people who can choose their priorities. But I have to work to make a living, so productivity *has* to be my priority. I don't have a choice." Quite frankly, we think this is a cop-out that people use to explain why they aren't living according to their values. Of course you have obligations, but you can still dream big and set your sights on making your life better. Simply having a job does not take that opportunity away from you. After all, even if you work a full-time job and sleep eight hours a night, you still have sixty-four extra hours left over each week to spend doing the things you want to do. We have yet to meet someone who, when really challenged, could not put aside an hour or two per week for themselves and their dreams—even if they were single working mothers. Remember, small changes can add up over time.

We encourage you to think big, and to rediscover the possibilities in your life. It's hard to dream about where you could be in a year if you are too focused on the concept of the daily grind at your job or too entrenched in the habit of working hard. Think instead about the things you could do to get you where you want to be in life. Thinking beyond today is the secret of many of our successful, entrepreneurial clients. Most started with little, but their passion was making a dream come alive. They built enterprises on next to nothing, but they possessed the tenacity, open-mindedness, flexibility, and resilience of those who have Affluence Intelligence. Although they experienced times of drudgery, failure, and loss, they persevered because, more than anything, they love to build, to grow an idea into a reality, to get people excited and working together toward a common goal. They have Affluence Intelligence because the process is more important than the product. Of course they enjoy making money. But their success is in how they build things, not how much money is in their bank accounts.

When it comes to affluence, far too many of us feel that our fantasies about a better or bigger life will never be realized, so we live our lives with "just good enough" expectations and attitudes, existing in our self-imposed psychological prison cells. We spend a lot of time looking toward others—life partners, family, jobs, communities, or governments—to find the key and release us. The good news is also the bad news: you have the key to the cell and the key to unlock your Affluence Intelligence by seeing a reality beyond your self-imposed prison cell. Being in your cell may be comfortable, but it is not living an affluent life. Familiarity may be comfortable, but it may also be your prison.

In order to guide you to most effectively responding to this part of the quiz, we have filled out the Lifestyles Priorities chart ourselves as an example.

STEPHEN'S LIFESTYLES PRIORITIES QUIZ

For his current productivity (work), Stephen gave a ranking of 1. (Joan agreed with his assessment. Remember, whenever possible, you want an objective second party to weigh in on your answers.) Productivity—whether it is his job, or other types—has a strong value for Stephen. It gives him a big emotional payoff—namely, the satisfaction of taking care of business. His parents were very hard-working people, and a work ethic was instilled in him at an early age.

People came in second, because he spends a lot of time every week with friends and family. Passion (being in nature, traveling, or playing the guitar) came next, at 3, because with his professional responsibilities he did not always have time for leisure activities. Joan said it was clear to her that passion was ranked way too low for Stephen. She pointed out that there would always be something to keep him from giving more time to them. This year, it was the exciting projects at work; next year it might be selling a real estate investment. Also, she reminded him that while he loved his work and might even feel passionate about it, passion as we are defining it means something more than just doing something you enjoy— it is doing the things that give you an almost physical high, that put you in the zone. Productivity (other) was ranked 4.

Peace and prosperity followed in the order of 5 and 6. These rankings were mostly based on the hours he spent on each activity per week.

Next Stephen had to consider the question, What would you like your average weekly activities to be one year from today? After some thought Stephen realized that peace could stay at its current rank position. However, he acknowledged that he would be happier if he made peace more of a priority at some time in the future.

On a practical level, this would mean making a commitment to a daily meditation practice, and working harder at being mindful to pause before reacting to a situation or to another person.

It was tricky for Stephen to decide what he was willing to change, because in order to make another one of the Ps his number one priority, he had to decrease productivity. (As we remind our clients, there are only so many hours in the day.) Stephen wanted to reduce the importance of productivity (work), giving him more time to pursue other priorities. Joan doubted that, with his work ethic, he would actually be able to reduce his work hours as much as he thought he could. When a person who knows you well gives feedback on how you have ranked your priorities, you have the opportunity to rethink and potentially revise the choice you have made. In this instance, her feedback had a sobering influence on his expectations of himself.

A big change was that Stephen felt that passion needed to become a higher priority. These passions included activities such as hiking, going to theatre and musical events, and playing the guitar. (Even when he left his band and became a psychologist, he held onto three guitars and two amps.) His passions also included traveling, which he has done at least seven weeks a year since he was twenty. In the next year, he planned to hike in the Tetons, snorkel in Hawaii, and visit South India (which he did!).

Stephen thought prosperity could remain at 6—his feelings had not changed about that priority. Joan disagreed. She said that Stephen spent so much time working that prosperity was more important, but he countered that it was the working itself—productivity—that he loved, not the money he made from it. Peace and passion were more important to him. In this case, Joan's challenge of Stephen's rank ordering of priorities helped Stephen gain greater certainty and clarity of the choices he had made.

As a man in his late fifties who has achieved a certain comfort with his money and lifestyle, Stephen is most interested in being challenged intellectually, sharing what he has learned in ways that have a real impact on others, and having time to do the things he truly loves to do.

Finally, Stephen had to acknowledge that he was not willing, over the next year, to decrease his productivity (work), because he had some exciting projects coming up. This is a crucial aspect of honestly ranking your priorities—bringing together the real and the ideal. While he was not able to change the rank of work productivity, he was able to see how he could reduce some of his time and energy in avocational pursuits, so he planned for a small decrease in productivity (other). While he wants to make much more time for his passions, and in the future would reduce his productivity in regard to work, Stephen realized, for the upcoming year, that he was willing to make relatively small shifts in his priorities.

Stephen's results are seen in Chart 3.1.

Stephen's score of 4 shows that where he is now and where he would like to be are not too different, and that he is mostly living according to his priorities. The higher the score, the more changes one has to make to be in alignment with one's priorities. The score in itself is neither good nor bad.

JOAN'S LIFESTYLE PRIORITIES QUIZ

Now it was time for Joan to take the quiz. Currently, productivity— whether it was in the form of work or other productive activity— was her number one priority. Joan is just naturally a productive person. Even without her work at the Money, Meaning & Choices Institute, she would still be highly productive. She loves to do

CHART 3.1   STEPHEN'S LIFESTYLE PRIORITIES

	Step 1: Today *Rank your current weekly activities in order of highest priority (1) through lowest priority (6)*	Step 2: One year from today *How you would like your weekly activities prioritized in one year in order of highest priority (1) through lowest priority (6)*	Step 3: Difference *Calculate the difference between steps 1 and 2*
PROSPERITY	6	6	0
PEOPLE	2	2	0
PRODUCTIVITY/WORK	1	1	0
PRODUCTIVITY/OTHER	4	5	1
PASSION	3	4	1
PEACE	5	3	2

	Step 4: Total Difference	*Add up the differences in step 3 to get your GAP number.*

GAP
Number = 4

projects whether at home, at work, or with friends. She wakes up in the morning full of energy, saying, "What projects do I really need and want to do today? What can I cross off my list today?" She actually has to limit herself as to how many projects she can work on. She has learned that her eyes are bigger than her stomach. Joan is powerfully motivated by accomplishing things, whether they earn her money or not. For this reason, in the future productivity can never go below a number 2 rank. She realized that she would have to reduce time spent on productivity (other) if she truly wanted to move up with the priorities of peace and passion, which had become more important to her as she reached midlife, and was completing the process of launching her children into college and self-sufficiency.

But passion also ranks high. Currently, it is third, although she would like to make it number two. Joan's greatest passion in life is dance; it is her religion. When it comes to her dance class, she is there come hell or high water. Nothing else takes precedence, and it is nonnegotiable that she goes dancing. Although in her younger years passion through dance ranked number one, she now had other important interests, given the choices she made through the years. In Joan's case, in contrast to Stephen's, adding up time spent each week dancing is not the only way she identifies her passion for dance because she works more than she dances. Instead, it is a clear demonstration of a high-priority activity in her nonworking hours.

Prosperity ranks lowest, currently and for the future. Like the rest of us, Joan would not mind having more money. It took her some soul-searching to realize that, while she would never say no to money, it was not actually a priority at this point in her life and career. Stephen suggested that maybe prosperity should be ranked higher, since with more prosperity she could delegate more chores to hired help and therefore free up more time for her passions. But Joan did not agree. She said that even if she married a millionaire, she would feel less stress (more peace) but would still be as productive as she is now, and her hourly schedule would probably not change all that much.

But peace is a bigger priority for her (number five). In order to gain more prosperity she would have to be more productive, and she is not sure she is willing to do that, because of what she would have to give up in her search for peace. Peace for Joan is reading a book in her hammock, working in her yard, being in nature, listening to music, or doing artwork. She also gets peace from dancing—but dancing is her passion, and this is an important distinction to make. Some of her peaceful activities are coupled with passion, and those priorities may therefore overlap, but that does not mean they are the same thing. It is important to recognize those activities that you are truly passionate about and how you do (or do not) make them a priority in your life.

Joan felt that although people had been second in the past, they should drop to third. Just because you downgrade a priority does not mean it is no longer important to you. For example, Joan is completely devoted to her children, and she loves the other people in her life, too. With her youngest about to go off to college, her children will not need her as much anymore. When she says she wants to make people less of a priority, she is talking about reducing social time with friends so she can spend more time dancing, as well as engaging in some peaceful productivity (other) activities, such as reading or gardening, that have moved up on her priority list. She is already putting this into practice, limiting lunches with friends from an hour and a half to forty-five minutes, and not doing them every two weeks but every four or six weeks. Joan's chart (Chart 3.2) shows her results.

Joan had a score of 4, which indicates the changes she wants to make. She is living in close alignment with her core values. And because her life reflects many of the elements of Affluence Intelligence, we might have expected this. However, despite the fact that she is so well versed in this information, she struggled with taking the test and is not sure that her answers may not change in the future (which they may well, because priorities naturally change as our lives change). For many of us, these scores will change as we

CHART 3.2   JOAN'S LIFESTYLE PRIORITIES

	Step 1: Today *Rank your current weekly activities in order of highest priority (1) through lowest priority (6)*	**Step 2: One year from today** *How you would like your weekly activities prioritized in one year in order of highest priority (1) through lowest priority (6)*	**Step 3: Difference** *Calculate the difference between steps 1 and 2*
PROSPERITY	6	6	0
PEOPLE	2	3	1
PRODUCTIVITY/WORK	1	1	0
PRODUCTIVITY/OTHER	4	5	1
PASSION	3	2	1
PEACE	5	4	1

Step 4: Total Difference   *Add up the differences in step 3 to get your GAP number.*

GAP Number = 4

age, and as our circumstances in life change. With her last child leaving for college, her priorities can change. In fact, she had to take time to really think through her priorities to make sure that her actions would be aligned with what is now most important for her.

Notice that both Joan and Stephen have ranked prosperity as number 6: they each really love what they do, and they don't do it solely for the money. They certainly enjoy money, especially as it makes their passions possible, but they are not particularly driven by it. Remember, affluence does not mean having a life that is primarily driven by making more money. Joan and Stephen have also seen how living their priorities and exercising the Affluence Intelligence attitudes and behaviors have led to life satisfaction that cannot be purchased. The challenge with this exercise is that you can get caught between the real and the ideal: if you can't imagine your ideal, you have no hope of getting there, but at the same time you must be realistic about what is possible. Joan also got tripped up in the blurring of the lines between her priorities. For example, the things that tap into her passions also give her peace. That is why it is important to take the time to think through different scenarios and make sure the choices you make are the choices you will live. Or, just as Joan and Stephen did the test together, do this with a friend who knows you very well, one who can point out what you may be forgetting or not have thought of.

You must allow yourself the time and space to really give this quiz careful thought. Ask yourself the following questions:

- To what extent do my daily life activities reflect this priority?
- To what extent am I willing to change something to have more of this priority in my life?

TEST YOURSELF

Now you are ready to take the Lifestyles Priorities Quiz. Think about where you are today, not where you were one, five, ten, or twenty years ago. Do your best to be completely honest about your priorities today, and what you would like them to be one year from now.

The smaller the difference between where you are today and where you would like to be in one year means you are living in alignment with your priorities. Be as objective as you can—remember, there is no judgment. If you can, go over the quiz with someone who knows you well and is not afraid to tell you the truth about yourself. You can also ask a close friend or your life partner to rank what they think your priorities are now, and what they believe you really want them to be one year from today. Then compare your answers to theirs, find the average, and record that number as your priority.

It is important when you take the test to separate the real from the ideal—that is, to think about what you are actually capable of doing and willing to do, versus what you might do in a perfect world. Remember that you can always come back and revise your numbers if you realize that your projection was too ambitious, or not ambitious enough, or if you realize that you are not willing to make certain changes after all. You might start with the ideal, but you must end up with the real.

Further, keep in mind that we are talking about your baseline, which is your average weekly experience. Of course, there will always be times when life takes an unexpected turn due to an illness, family obligation, or other work or life crisis. Finally, and most importantly, be aware that an activity may seem to fall under more than one priority. If you encounter overlapping priorities, you will simply have to tease out which one is the more important. For example, Stephen's productivity (work) makes him happy. One could argue that it also makes him peaceful and passionate. But his work does not fall under the category of peace or passion—it is productivity. Instead, peace for him is hiking, and meditation and passion is going to the theatre, learning new things, and playing guitar. Very few activities or experiences in life are one thing only, and chances are there will be some overlap in the things that are important to you. You must be careful to recognize what is the *primary* function of that activity in your life.

A WORD ABOUT PRIORITIES
AND SOCIAL PRESSURES

You must also be careful in ranking your priorities to be sure that you are designating something as a priority because it is what you actually want and not because it is something that is expected of you. For example, women in particular often have a challenge when it comes to ranking people as a priority. Most women are somewhat burdened by the amount of relationships they have (while many men want to have more). Women commonly cater to so many other people that they do not cater to themselves. If this is true of you, then taking this test can be an eye-opener. If you are a woman who cares for others (and virtually all women do), take a moment to recognize what effect societal expectations have on you. In what ways do those social expectations (and use of your time) keep you from passion, peace, productivity (work), or prosperity?

Women also tend to have many extra household duties that may seem small, but they add up, so if you are ranking by time spent, you can get a skewed rank. Even women who work full time are expected to be the ones to sweep the kitchen floor. Statistics show the percentage of time women spend on housework is much greater than the time men spend (whether the women work full time or not). Therefore, the fact is that productivity (other)—that is, cleaning house—is expected of her, and because she lives up to that expectation, productivity might be ranked higher than she might like.

Or a woman who is caring for both children and elderly parents may feel that productivity (other) is nonnegotiable, because somebody has to do the caretaking—and if not her, then who?

While women have challenges in this area, men have them, too. For example, a man working in commercial real estate might have a secret yearning that tugs at his soul—to be a sculptor, writer, or maker of fine furniture. But because of societal expectations, he must suppress this urge in an attempt to forget and deny its importance. As a result, he may carry a deep sadness and sense that life is passing him by.

Now is the time to bring forth your true desires and to acknowledge them without judgment. You must ask yourself, "Am I ranking this as a priority because other people expect it of me, or am I ranking it because in my heart of hearts I feel it is what you truly want?" At the end of the day, are you tired of taking care of other people, or of working a job that provides for your family, but leaves you feeling empty? If so, be honest with yourself, even if you are not ready to share this information with others or to act upon it.

AFFLUENCE INTELLIGENCE AND YOUR MARRIAGE

If you are married or in a committed relationship, you are not living in a vacuum; your spouse's or partner's Affluence Intelligence Quotient and habits about spending, saving, and sharing money affect you, and vice versa.

When it comes to affluence, there are a number of ways people are drawn to their partners. Often, we are attracted to people with very similar Affluence Intelligence Quotient profiles to our own, because we feel most comfortable when we are with people who feel the same way about finances that we do. This marriage or partnership of sameness creates a sense of security. Having the same beliefs about spending, saving, and sharing money can make a couple feel united in their values and goals. However, they will also probably share the same Affluence Intelligence vulnerabilities. The relationship is more likely to get stuck in a particular pattern of spending or saving, which will seem normal to each partner but may actually be dysfunctional. It is harder for people in such relationships to gain a sense of balance because they have no one to bump up against or provide an alternative perspective. For example, a saver and a spender have to come to terms with their financial picture and can gain new perspectives from one another more readily than the couple who share the same financial lens.

On the opposite end of the spectrum, it is possible to have a marriage of opposites, because opposites attract, both in love and in money. Because having money is often seen as being sexy, many people enter into romantic relationships for financial reasons. Traditional marriage, in which the man provides financially and the woman oversees care of the home and child rearing, is a clear example of this arrangement, although a man may also find a woman who is appealing because of her wealth. The partner who is wealthier or more successful may enjoy basking in the admiration of his or her partner and feel empowered and loved.

For some couples, this works very well. As long as they can agree on a budget and lifestyle that are acceptable to both of them and respect each other's differences, they can usually create a solid foundation for their relationship.

For other couples, the fantasy of how "opposites attract" can backfire. For example, consider those relationships in which one partner is a spender and the other a saver. The spender will eventually resent the ways in which the saver judges and attempts to control his or her actions. The saver may end up feeling disregarded and out of control, feeling that she or he has partnered with a person who is immature and impulsive about money. Unless this dynamic is effectively managed, these differing financial styles can derail an otherwise good relationship.

Because attitudes about affluence can have a major impact on a relationship, it can be very helpful for both people in a couple to take the Lifestyles Priorities Quiz, and then compare the results. With the profile in hand, the couple is better able to establish shared values and an action plan.

Now it is time to fill out the Lifestyles Priorities chart for yourself.

CHART 3.3   YOUR LIFESTYLE PRIORITIES

	Step 1: Today *Rank your current weekly activities in order of highest priority (1) through lowest priority (6)*	Step 2: One year from today *How you would like your weekly activities prioritized in one year in order of highest priority (1) through lowest priority (6)*	Step 3: Difference *Calculate the difference between steps 1 and 2*
PROSPERITY			
PEOPLE			
PRODUCTIVITY/WORK			
PRODUCTIVITY/OTHER			
PASSION			
PEACE			

Step 4: Total Difference   *Add up the differences in step 3 to get your GAP number.*

GAP Number =

SCORING YOUR LIFESTYLE PRIORITIES

A gap of 0–2   40 points

A gap of 3–5   35 points

A gap of 6–8   30 points

A gap of 9–11   25 points

A gap of 12–13   20 points

A gap of 14 or greater   15 points

TOTAL PART A SCORE: _____ out of a possible 40
(Transfer this score to page 154, so you can
obtain your total AIQ score).

chapter four

BEHAVIORS AND ATTITUDES OF THE AFFLUENT

*I*n our work as consultants on money and meaning, over and over again we have seen that people who have unlocked their Affluence Intelligence behave in very different ways from those who have not. They have not only the right attitude but also the key behavioral skills that naturally propel them forward in their journey to affluence. Like the rest of us, the affluent are not perfect. But they know how to use their attitudes and behavioral skills to attain financial security and happiness overall.

BEHAVIORS

Many of the following behaviors will already be familiar to you. But for you to unlock your Affluence Intelligence, you will need to better develop and more fully exercise these behaviors.

Resilience

People with Affluence Intelligence are resilient. We all make mistakes and experience setbacks, but the affluent react differently when things do not go as they had hoped. They might feel discouraged for a moment, but then they rally. They don't give up. Like baseball players, they may have a thousand strikeouts, but they keep playing and eventually hit a home run. Research at the University of Pennsylvania has found that resilience is essential to success and happiness, whether the issue is parenting, school achievement, work productivity, or performing at one's peak ability as an athlete.[1]

Our client Charlene is a good example of overcoming an adverse situation. Given her terrible background, other people might have said, "My life has been truly horrible. I have been a victim of child abuse and domestic violence. I've got the scorecard to justify saying, I give up." But Charlene always taps into a never-ending source of energy that keeps her moving forward. Like many of our clients who make lemonade out of lemons, she finds the resilience to rebound from her personal and professional problems.

This does not mean that she is out of touch with her feelings. When things go wrong, she gets angry, sad, or frustrated like most of us. She doesn't enjoy setbacks, but she doesn't let them derail her, either. For example, although she has gone through bariatric surgery and lost a tremendous amount of weight, she struggles to keep it off. Despite all of her efforts, she still suffers from the negative judgments of others (and also, at times, from the voice inside her head that says, "I should be thirty pounds lighter"). In addition, she has a series of serious health issues that repeatedly impair her ability to function, and, on occasion, threaten her life. Does she get tired of it? You bet. But instead of throwing in the towel, she picks herself up and goes on with her life.

Our clients with Affluence Intelligence have a very special quality of resilience: they are very efficient at handling conflict and at quickly making changes in response to any setbacks. They learn from trial and error without wasting time, getting stuck, or taking too many detours. As one of our clients recently said, "I am not religious about any of my traits." What she means is that she is open to changing her attitudes or viewpoints if it makes sense to do so, and she does not feel a need to maintain a way of behaving or thinking if she hears of a better alternative. Those with Affluence Intelligence "roll with the punches," see adversity as a challenge, and often turn it into a learning experience. In our work with affluent people we have witnessed some key behaviors that fall under the umbrella of resilience, including:

Knowing When to Cut Your Losses

One of our clients told us, "I will walk through walls to make things happen," but he also knows when it's time to move on. This ability to know when you are banging your head against a wall versus making progress on taking the wall down is crucial. The affluent are aware that they have choices—and sometimes the best choice is to quit. They will handle rejection and failure with aplomb, but they understand when the world is giving them feedback—even when that feedback is that it's time to give up.

We have seen this change in our clients in an almost physical way. Stephen commented, "I can practically see their brains change. They stop, they think, and then they look up and say, 'Okay, this isn't working well; I'm going to give up that [behavior or situation]' It's not that they don't struggle to reach this decision, or that they don't feel pain or disappointment, but they have told us, 'I don't want to fall into a victim mentality, and I hate feeling trapped, like there is nothing I can do.' Instead they say, 'I know I feel like I am trapped right now, but I have the keys to get out.' Over and over, we see them use their keys to escape from a situation that is holding them back."

Making a conscious decision to let go or get out of a situation that is not working and not moving you forward is very different from simply giving up or quitting when the going gets tough. The first is empowering; the second is disempowering.

For example: Buckley, a real estate investor, spends time and money on projects that frequently have a long initial phase of development before breaking ground. During this period, Buckley would bring together the efforts of architects, engineers, community groups, regulatory agencies, and other investors. He would invest a good deal of his energy into these projects, keeping a positive attitude, navigating obstacles while rallying the troops. Because of the complexity involved, it was not a surprise when the occasional project ended before construction began. Buckley would work hard on his projects until, as he put it, "I knew it was time to turn the switch off." He would wind the project down, dust himself off, and then rapidly move on to the next opportunity. He understood that his and others' hard work were not necessarily enough for success—that a percentage of failure was part of his chosen business enterprise. Buckley had made a conscious decision to let go, staying in charge of the process.

This is unlike the experience when cutting your losses results in feeling like a personal failure, or wraps you in seemingly endless self-dialogue of nonconstructive review and regret. Or when a person refuses to let go, even in the face of clear defeat. We are reminded of a dentist who wanted to build a chain of dental services in shopping malls. He got a couple of other dentist-investors and they opened up "dentists in a box" stores in a few malls in their state. The first year looked promising, but as they tried to expand, they were not able to raise sufficient capital. Also, a larger corporation had begun to roll out a similar business concept, with television advertising they couldn't afford. One of his partners dropped out, but our client the dentist did not want to give up. He mortgaged his own home (representing half of his retirement savings) to help fund the business. By the third year, the business was showing diminishing returns. He was working twice as hard and making about the same amount of income as when he was in solo practice. His remaining business partner pressed to sell the business, but our client refused. He believed that, "It was all a matter of time. . . . We will either be purchased by a bigger company, or we will gain traction on our own." Yes, it was good that he really believed in the quality of their services, but it was bad that he couldn't see how much of his self-esteem was on the line. When his borrowing against his Keogh retirement plan threatened to destroy his remaining savings, his wife had had enough. Her leaving was his wakeup call.

The Ability to "Get Over It"

The social stigma of getting psychological help has diminished over the past few decades, which is wonderful. Unfortunately, at the same time, something unexpected has happened: Many people who have been in counseling or therapy get caught in the trap of not using what they have learned to heal and go forward in their lives. They have gotten stuck trying to discover what is wrong and have not paid enough attention to the next step—making changes. Moving beyond issues into action is what psychoanalysts call "working through" or bringing together what is known (psychological awareness) with taking action: taking initiatives and risks that will produce changes in self-perception and behavior. For a person to resolve his or her issues, whether an addiction, childhood abuse, or obesity, he or she must not only understand the root of its causes, but achieve a degree of acceptance and move on.

As we have seen again and again in the lives of our clients, moving on means stopping the endless cycles of ambivalence, knowing when you have suffered enough, understanding the issues enough, and allowing guilt to dissipate. Moving on means achieving recovery and not making your problems your lifelong identity. This does not mean that a person does not have residual feelings about an emotionally complex issue, but, rather than continuing to ruminate about the problem, they take lessons from their experience and chart a new course. As Stephen is fond of saying, "The data is in. We understand it well enough. It is time to use what we've learned in new life experiences." For example, a man who has frustrations in finding the right person to marry—which he understands has to do in part with old feelings of being controlled by his mother— might lead him to embrace an identity as a "walking wounded" bachelor who will be forever ambivalent about commitment. By following the tenet of resilience as part of his Affluence Intelligence, however, he would use what he knows about himself and his approach to relationships to change the way he relates to women so that he can deepen a connection with his partner, rather than to simply replay the past.

A Willingness to Learn From Your Mistakes

Our client Dennis had a problem with anxiety, which tripped him up in the workplace, and he came to us for help to reduce it. After talking to him, we discovered that he occasionally drank too much. The day following a drinking bout he felt like he might throw up or faint, and he also felt very anxious. He was worried about his health and worried about how badly he felt the next day or two after drinking. We had him go to a doctor to rule out medical issues, and then, although he loved to drink, he decided to reduce the number of drinks he would have on any occasion. And then he did it. He did not become defensive or deny that there was a problem; he saw that he was making a mistake, and was willing to learn from it and make changes accordingly.

Being willing to learn from your mistakes shows that you hold learning as a core value, even when it means acknowledging a serious personal problem, or acknowledging a decision you made that did not work out. Rather than getting defensive or saving face, those with high Affluence Intelligence value learning and correcting course. David, the architect, knew that the path he had taken was not right for him, but he had a hard time heeding the lesson. Instead, he found himself slipping into a depression about how stuck he was, and how he had made choices in the past that were no longer right for him.

Assertiveness

People who have unlocked their Affluence Intelligence know what they want, say what they want, and go after what they want. They speak in a straightforward and unapologetic manner and in a way that politely but firmly demands recognition of their rights, even when they anticipate that others will object to what they are asking for. They know that in order to get what they want, they need to make sure that they communicate those wants clearly and unequivocally.

At the heart of assertiveness is a healthy sense of entitlement— sufficient self-esteem to feel that you deserve to be treated well. Whether you send a steak back at a restaurant because it is too rare, or if you insist on the discount on your hotel bill that you were promised, this demonstrates that you have reasonable and healthy expectations about how you should be treated by others (as well as how you treat them). Unhealthy entitlement is often expressed in aggressive behavior, which is completely different from assertiveness. Aggressive and selfish behavior have no part in Affluence Intelligence.

Being assertive is not always easy. One of our clients told us, "I really had to muster up the courage before I could tell my wife what I wanted (to live overseas with her for a year, given a promising job opportunity), because I knew it was not going to go over well and I was worried that it might threaten the relationship." But he did it. He simply said, "I am seriously considering living overseas for a year and want to help you understand my wants and needs. I want to be happy, and want you to know that while what I want may not be exactly what you had in mind, I needed to tell you, and I want to work it out together." He was clear and assertive about what he wanted and why. Much to his surprise, his wife eventually agreed to what he wanted. He expressed his needs, but also let his wife know that he respected her different point of view, and ultimately wanted to make a decision that would strengthen their marriage, not result in an endless power struggle.

When you take a stand with someone, he or she may not be happy about it and may try to fight you. Don't let this deter you. Know also that the worst thing that can happen if you ask for something is that the other person will say no. But there is a chance of getting what you want if you ask, and virtually no chance at all if you don't. As Joan says, "It's about asserting yourself gracefully, saying what you want and need in ways that make it more likely for others to hear you."

Becoming assertive takes practice, and is always more of a challenge when it comes to issues of love, autonomy, and intimacy.

However, when you unlock your Affluence Intelligence and become assertive when dealing with these kinds of issues, the payoff can be huge. At its best, assertiveness is a way of thinking and behaving that allows a person to stand up for his or her rights while respecting the rights of others. Beyond expressing one's rights, assertiveness increases honest and open communication, which benefits both the individual and his or her relationships.

Interpersonal Effectiveness

Whether you are at home or at work, being interpersonally effective means being successful when interacting with others. You are able to read the emotions of other people, and communicate your own. You are able to establish and maintain relationships, connect on a personal level, and be sensitive to the well-being of others. The affluent use their emotional intelligence (as defined in the well-known book *Emotional Intelligence* by Daniel Goleman) to be personally effective.

If you are effective at work, you are more likely to create alliances with your colleagues and achieve results. At home, you may be better able to maintain a happy marriage or to have a good relationship with your children and in your friendships. Those with Affluence Intelligence value teamwork, harnessing the power of it to reach both their goals and the goals they share with others. A single-minded, strong-willed individual can go very far, but a person who can relate well with others can take a rocket ship to greatness.

Contrary to the conventional view that entrepreneurs are self-centered individuals who fly solo, most of our clients are amazingly great team builders, team leaders, and team players. Not in just one of these roles, but in all of these roles. When interpersonal effectiveness is unlocked, your emotional intelligence, social credibility, and social effectiveness are all running at 100 percent. When we think of visionary and effective leaders, we think of individuals who can communicate effectively and draw people together to meet a common objective. We've seen it in Silicon Valley start-ups, in retail business ventures, and in large traditional companies. We've also seen it in smaller but equally important ways, in parenting children and developing personal relationships. The interpersonal effectiveness of those with Affluence Intelligence is their emotional intelligence in action, always striving to improve personal and professional relationships and to achieve better outcomes.

An Ability to Work Hard and Achieve Goals

When people with Affluence Intelligence really throw themselves into what they want to do, they usually have a goal of wealth in mind, but they love the ride whether they become wealthy or not. They are not primarily concerned with striving for a particular a financial goal—instead, they are focused on setting a complete life strategy goal.

For example, Amy's goal was to be exposed to and learn about leading-edge ideas and culture, and to interact with movers and shakers in the business and cultural communities. She needed money to attend thought-leadership conferences, but money was only a tool for her, not an end point. Her personality, energy, and zeal for life were also tools that she could use to achieve her goals, make money, and enjoy herself along the way.

Anyone can talk about a strategy or write out a mission statement about their goals, but affluent people *take concrete action and follow through by doing what they have said they will do.* As professionals, we can rapidly tell whether a person has Affluence Intelligence, or is just a talker by how they speak about achieving their goals. Many of us know people who say they are planning to lose weight—you can judge their level of commitment by whether they say, "I really should lose twenty pounds, but boy do I love chocolate cake," or, "I am going to lose twenty pounds by the end of the year. I have thrown out all of my junk food and hired a personal trainer."

Truly affluent people work very hard, and follow through on their commitments. Even our very wealthy clients who never have to work another day in their lives have worked very, very hard to get to the point where they no longer have to work for their money. You can work hard and not be affluent (and many low-wage workers do), but it is almost impossible to be affluent without hard work. There is no getting around the power of having a plan and putting in the hours needed to achieve your goals.

Those who have not unlocked their Affluence Intelligence often don't like to accept hard work as a key to affluence. They are likely to say about a rich person, "He got lucky." Our clients will openly admit that they have been lucky. But luck alone will not yield true affluence. Consider Howard, the successful appliance store owner. He put in many hours at his office, but even more hours in community efforts that indirectly marketed and supported his core business. He enjoyed these activities, but he was also aware of how important they were to maintaining and growing his wealth.

Persistence

The affluent, when they set a goal and have calculated the risk, are willing to keep going until they get what they want. They persist beyond the point when others would have given up. They have the capacity to stick to a task until they achieve their goal.

For example, a salesperson may make ninety-one calls and get ninety noes before he or she gets one yes. But they keep going until they get that yes. They understand that if they give up after a few rejections then they will never get to yes. They are willing to put in the hard work, to keep going even in the face of difficulty. If they make a commitment to any endeavor (such as, I am going to learn to cook), they keep it. They actually do what they say they are going to do.

Joan's mother, when given a cancer diagnosis, did not collapse and give up. She made the cancer part of her life, but not all of her life, and she kept going. She went to chemo, but she also went boogie boarding. She persevered.

The affluent understand that there will be ups and downs, but a roadblock or a challenge is seen as something to overcome, to go around, or to go over—not something that will stop them. They assume that there will be setbacks on their journey, but they will not allow them to prevent their journey from continuing. (This is very different from simply not knowing when to give up, continuing on out of stubbornness, not listening to clear signals or hoping the individual will make a radical personality shift that is unhealthy persistence that can send you down the wrong path.) The affluent abide by one of our favorite lines from the *I Ching*, the ancient Chinese book that is both an oracle and coach: "Perseverance furthers."

ATTITUDES

Attitudes are based upon our positive or negative feelings, beliefs, and predispositions, about ourselves and toward others and life situations.

Optimism

People with Affluence Intelligence typically assume that they will succeed. They believe that they are going to achieve the best possible result in any given situation. We have seen clients who are distraught about the failure of a marriage or the fact that their business is going belly up, and yet they trust that everything is eventually going to be okay. At the end of the day, they believe that life is essentially good, and that an optimistic attitude will provide better direction and a better outcome than a pessimistic attitude.

It helps if you are naturally an optimistic person, but if you are not, don't despair. Affluent people do not wake up feeling happy and optimistic every day. But they tell us that they would rather think positively than anticipate the worst. An optimistic attitude can be learned, although we will caution you that there is such a thing as being overly optimistic. Optimism will help unlock Affluence Intelligence when it is tempered by what psychologists call "reality testing"—that is, the ability to distinguish what is real from what is fantasy. If one's optimism is overly driven by fantasy, it may not produce concrete, positive outcomes. There are people who seem to be eternally optimistic and who perennially wear rose-colored glasses, but never really get anywhere.

We are struck by people who have the stellar capacity to negotiate the best compromise possible between the real and the ideal, without overly restricting or diminishing either. Timothy was a very successful venture capitalist who was known for his ability to know when to get in and when to get out of the market. We remember sitting in his lovely home in Greenwich, Connecticut, looking out at the changing colors in his backyard. Timothy was telling us about a business opportunity he was considering in Amsterdam. Stephen asked him, "How do you know this is the right thing to do? You're an expert at taking these kinds of risks; what is your secret?"

Timothy leaned forward and said, "Look: everyone pays attention to the one or two big successes I've had. Few pay attention to the dozen bad choices I've made. I do the analytical part of the work very carefully. I have the best people helping me. I use my optimism about business to see the possibilities, and I let my advisors argue against me. We review the details, we slug it out, and make no decisions. The next morning I wake up, see how I feel about the deal, and make a decision. I have learned, over the course of many years, that my batting average will be good enough to stay in the game. And I've been lucky: look around at this place. I've got a good life, and I'm grateful. But this is not a game for people who cannot remain positive in the face of adversity."

Much to our surprise, Timothy told us that he did not want his children to follow in his footsteps. He said that being a private equity venture capitalist is a hard road to financial success. But he also told us, "Win or lose, I absolutely love to play the game!"

Optimism embodies hope, as well as the belief there can be a positive outcome, even when things that you have planned go sideways. Sometimes life gets in the way of the best of plans. We cannot control all of the outside forces that operate on us, but we can determine how we will adapt and grow with the consequences.

Stan, at age forty, lost a job he had held (and done very well at) for more than ten years. Prior to being let go, he had been reassured that he was too vital to cut, but when the company was forced to downsize, he was out. He had a wife, a child, and little money in the bank. For the first month, Stan was shocked, hurt, and angry. After looking for a similar job for a few months and not finding a position, he was scared and getting depressed. In his work with us, he quickly saw that he needed to not let his anger about the job loss get in the way of what he needed to learn to take the best next steps. By stepping outside of his frustration and disappointment, Stan rediscovered his natural sense of optimism and hope for the future. He came to see that a large part of his difficulty was that his entire area of expertise had been downsized in companies across the country. He came up with a new plan: look for independent contracting positions rather than regular employment, because outsourcing his expertise seemed to have become the "new normal." It paid off. He got two contracting jobs, and two years later, had two contractors working for him. Within five years, his business had expanded to an income level well beyond that of his previous employment.

Risk Taking

Risk takers do not worry about failing. Instead, they are focused on the possibilities. The successful clients of ours (such as salespeople) say, "Okay, I've failed a few times." They don't take it personally, and they don't let it trip them up. They don't see themselves as victims; they see what they can learn and keep going. Many worry about failing, or worry about being ashamed or looking bad, that they stop themselves from taking risks that make sense—a calculated risk that weighs the odds and crunches the numbers is very different from taking a blind gamble. When you unlock Affluence Intelligence, taking *calculated* risks becomes part of your life navigational system.

Taking risks does not always end well, but people with Affluence Intelligence understand this and are not derailed when their risk taking does not pay off. They learn from the risks that did not work out and use that information to be better prepared for the next time. Our clients who are successful entrepreneurs have a need for risk taking the way most of us have a need for security. They will find opportunities to use their capacity to calculate risks and take initiatives, whether they need the money or not. They love the learning curve, and those who have become very wealthy love to build *a ladder of calculated risks,* in which each step is built upon what is learned from the success of the prior step. By staying in touch with what is real, and having the courage to go forward and without overthinking things, they can rapidly build an enterprise where others might still be anxiously wondering if they should or should not take the plunge.

As the manager of a hardware store that had long been in his family, Brian saw that people shopped in his store the same way they might in a large pharmacy: they came for one thing and walked out with three. The store where he worked had the look and feel of a classic hardware store, and Brian felt he could do better. So he took a risk: He took out a massive loan to set up a "new concept" venture, a hardware store that would have the look and feel of a large regional pharmacy, and have appliances and other home furnishings that were usually found only in large department stores. The risk paid off. Within one year, the store was selling almost as many nonhardware items as hardware; within three years, the nonhardware items accounted for 70 percent of sales. Brian was happy, but not content. He knew that if they didn't grow rapidly, another large box store enterprise would come in and take over. So he again took out a substantial loan (the collateral was his existing business, not personal assets) and took the risk of starting three more stores. Seven years later, he was in charge of a chain of these stores and planning his retirement exit strategy.

Those with Affluence Intelligence may be so driven to take risks that, at times, they will go forward even when the potential consequences of the risk are not as comfortable as they would like. As Peter told us: "As a hard-core entrepreneur, I don't feel like I take risks. It feels like I have done the research and that the odds of being successful are better than what most people would define as risky. The most significant risk I took was when I bought a well-known, successful ski film company. I was too young and inexperienced to fully understand what I was doing, the level of the risk involved, and the significance of the debt I was personally guaranteeing. However, given all that, with what I know now, rationally I would argue it would be too risky a thing to do. I was lucky, and I would absolutely do it again."

Curiosity and Open-mindedness

The people we have worked with who have unlocked their Affluence Intelligence are curious about the world, and they use that curiosity as a way to find solutions to whatever problems they may be facing. They are always looking to learn, especially about themselves. Those who have not fully unlocked this capacity may be curious about themselves, too, but they are reluctant, or simply do not *act* on what they learn. The ability to take action is crucial.

Curiosity is infectious and can make you stimulating, fun, and engaging. For example, Ron became very interested in alternative energy. While he knew little about the field, he believed that he could create a financially lucrative future in it. So he spoke to people installing solar panels, to wind turbine engineers, to businesspeople who were evaluating alternative energy companies, and to people at his local utility company. He wanted to know about others' point of view, their expertise, and their experience. His attitude opened door after door, ultimately resulting in his investment in, as he told us, "a completely new and exciting form of alternative energy." By engaging people in conversations, Ron showed them that he was truly interested in what they did and what they thought. Without a doubt, everybody wants that kind of attention. For Ron, this was not a sales tactic. He was truly curious—not just about himself, but about others.

Curiosity, combined with real respect for those you speak with, shows your desire to learn. As Joan puts it, our clients want to hear the wisdom of others. Everyone loves to tell their story, and to express what they know. By being respectfully curious (rather than aggressively curious)—or, as some say, endlessly curious—the speaker is invited into a relationship: to share information, and to potentially be a partner or team member. This approach opens doors and expands social networks. Most people respond positively to this kind of genuine curiosity and don't feel the need to protect themselves, feel competitive, or to close up. Instead, they feel an interest and curiosity of their own and respond accordingly.

The affluent are open-minded. They may resist a new idea at first (as we all can), but eventually they say, "Oh, that's something new! Maybe I need to consider it." Their interest in improving themselves is stronger than their fear of being judged, their fear of change, or their fear of being wrong. Our clients don't make the assumption that the new idea is a negative judgment about what they know or are doing. They are eager to learn, they want to see possibilities, and they are always open to a new opportunity.

Advances in understanding brain functioning and development help shed light on these abilities. A brain that is flexible and open to new learning (known as "neuroplasticity") is a brain that will adapt and function very well as we age. Our clients who have unlocked Affluence Intelligence have brain plasticity, as we all do, but our clients believe in their ability to make changes, and use this capacity to their advantage, which means that any time they do something different or look at things differently, they can increase their neuroplasticity. We find it exciting that the brain can grow and change in response to new experiences, allowing us to change and develop at any point in our lives.

Groundbreaking new research suggests that the human brain is able to generate entirely new brain cells, and that it is able to do this even later in life, at age seventy and beyond. Thus, the adage "use it or lose it" is very important to cultivating neuroplasticity and growth. Skills that have been lost can be relearned, the decline of abilities can be staved off or reversed, and entirely new functions can, potentially, be gained.

The "grooves" in your brain that reflect known patterns can be changed with the repetition of new thoughts and behaviors. Scientific studies have proven something that we have seen repeatedly in the lives of our truly successful clients, regardless of their age: people can change their brain functioning. As you begin developing greater open-mindedness, and increasing your neuroplasticity, you will unlock Affluence Intelligence. It takes work, but it can happen.

There are numerous ways to exercise this capacity to rewire your brain and to increase your open-mindedness. Many of our very wealthy clients, in their seventies and early eighties, continue going to conferences and events. They love being stimulated, keeping themselves (and their brains) active, and, in particular, learning about things they know little about. This curiosity and open-mindedness is a powerful component of unlocking Affluence Intelligence. At a conference for very wealthy families (to gain entry, a person had to have at least $100 million in investable assets), Joan and Stephen gave a talk on the psychology of money and control. At the end of the talk, a man in his mid-eighties came up to Stephen and said, "Thank you so much. I really had little idea about how my money could result in my grandchildren feeling controlled by me and being unmotivated. I've made some mistakes, and I want to change some things. I've taken pages of notes, which I will carefully review when I get home." Stephen was stunned by his genuine curiosity and open-mindedness. Earlier, not knowing who he was other than somebody's delightful grandfather, Stephen had playfully chatted with this man during a coffee break. Stephen later learned that he was the patriarch of a multi-billion dollar family business (with a name that all of us know) who had succeeded beyond his humble upbringing, and beyond his wildest dreams.

A Willingness to Change

People with Affluence Intelligence can tolerate the anxiety and uncertainty that naturally comes with change. They also understand that change doesn't happen overnight. When you're trying to change—whether starting a new exercise plan, or learning a new skill—it's normal to wander off the mark, and then bring yourself back on target.

Most people change as a consequence of negative motivations—namely, pain and fear. If you are neither in pain nor fearful, then you need to make a conscious choice to change. Until you unlock the capacity to choose to change, you may be among those who hate change. It is normal to ask, "If I change, what will happen to me?" Unfortunately, many of us focus too much on the possible negative repercussions of any changes we may envision. In contrast, the affluent see change as an opportunity. Even if they get blindsided by a spouse suddenly saying, "I want a divorce," the affluent understand that unwelcome change can be an opportunity for potential positive outcomes, depending on how it is handled.

As psychologists, we understand that welcoming change is often easier said than done, because the brain loves the familiar. Homeostasis—the impulse to maintain equilibrium—is a biological and psychological mechanism that brings us comfort. In fact, the brain loves predictable patterns, even when they are bad patterns. Take, for example, dieting. Those who struggle with their weight might eat a chocolate chip cookie while knowing full well that they will regret it later. Yet eating sweets is their familiar and comfortable pattern, so they still eat that cookie day after day, month after month, and year after year.

But having the ability to change, enabling successful adaptation and growth, is vital to unlocking our Affluence Intelligence. The good news is that we really can change, even after a lifetime of habitual and comfortable behaviors. Unfortunately, change brings discomfort, and most of us do not like to feel uncomfortable—it's simply human nature. We all have our comfort zones, and we like to stay in them. If you choose a life in which you stubbornly insist on maintaining the comfort of the known rather than experiencing the discomfort of change, you may find yourself chained to your familiar, inhibiting patterns. For example, this dynamic can be seen in people's spending, saving, and sharing patterns. Whether good or bad, take notice of how spenders tend to remain spenders, savers remain savers, and how a person's income level (with the exception of the time after a layoff) tends to remain the same. When you move away from the familiar and the comfortable and stop colluding with comfort, your chance to become more affluent greatly increases.

Those who have unlocked Affluence Intelligence are willing to make difficult choices and to take uncomfortable risks. They move outside their comfort zones in order to make things happen, and this psychological risk taking is crucial to success.

A Sense of Control Over One's Life

Perhaps you know someone who regularly says, "I have to work at a job I hate. I don't have any choice in the matter. I will never find a job that I really enjoy." They go on to tell you that they are a victim of their circumstances. In some ways, they may be correct. Certainly, social and economic forces outside the self are powerful variables. Unemployment, a poor economy, poverty, or lack of economic or educational opportunities can make anyone feel that the deck is stacked against them. But they may take it further and build a case for feeling powerless, and not in control of their lives, and blame others for their problems. This was the plight of David, our architect, who felt his life was on a treadmill (driven by social and familial expectations) that was being run at ever increasing speeds, and that the best he could do was to (exhaustingly) keep running.

Having a sense of personal agency, of knowing that you are in the driver's seat of your life, and that you have control over your thoughts, feelings, and actions, is at the core of those who have unlocked Affluence Intelligence. Life is not something that happens to them, nor is it a set of circumstances over which they are ultimately powerless. They focus on how they can take action; they see themselves as able to regulate their feelings and impulses, and are empowered to make choices.

You may not feel in control every minute of your life, but ultimately increasing your affluence is about seeing yourself as having the ability and power to be in control of your attitude and your actions in response to their circumstances.

Many think the simple answer is that those with the money have the power in this world. Certainly, money creates opportunities and offers choices, but we don't have to go any further than the evening news to see that rich people (or people with political clout, or celebrity status) can act powerless and use their wealth in self-destructive ways. Having money does not automatically give people a sense of agency, self-control, and empowerment. This is the paradox and also the core truth of Affluence Intelligence—you can be rich, but not affluent.

In contrast, those with Affluence Intelligence see that they are the actors in their lives, rather than the reactors. They are solution oriented. They say, "As the person in control of my life, it is up to me to find a solution to whatever problem I am facing." Even when external circumstances are dire, they value their ability to be in charge of their feelings, thoughts, impulses, and actions. When Melissa's portfolio radically dropped during the Great Recession, she, like so many others, had lost half of her savings. Her financial advisors tried to reassure her but did not offer any solutions that sounded good to her. Instead, she took responsibility for her situation and looked for opportunities in the downturn. She had been in real estate a decade before, and used her knowledge to find, buy, and rehab derelict properties that were near colleges or corporate centers, because she knew that people needed affordable housing near where they went to school or worked. She targeted boarded-up properties that she bought for very little cash; the banks were happy to get this "bad paper" off their books. She used some of her own money, and borrowed money from others. She successfully completed one project, rented it out, and then moved on to do two more.

By taking control of a situation that had unexpectedly and rapidly spiraled downward, Melissa slowly but surely rebuilt her nest egg. Like anyone who had lost half of his or her savings, she was scared, but she knew that no one else would rescue her. Of course, some things happen to us that are truly out of our control, such as a frightening medical diagnosis. We might get cancer, or multiple sclerosis, or develop a brain tumor. People with Affluence Intelligence do the very best they can with the cards they are dealt. We are not in control of what happens to us, but we are in control of our response to it.

Psychological Mindedness

Being psychologically minded means that you have the ability to think about and recognize your psychological workings, and that you can reflect upon yourself. This ability helps people step back and consider their choices. It provides a necessary pause between having an impulse and taking action.

The affluent are mindful of themselves, and they make conscious choices. They use this skill to manage their experiences, and to better understand what they are willing or not willing to do to reach a goal. They work on seeing themselves objectively, to make critical and honest appraisals of their own shortcomings, and are not ruled by unconscious motivations for what they do. Having the ability to step back from their direct experience, they can then recognize their nonproductive behaviors and decisions.

There has been a revolution of interest in the capacity of psychological mindfulness in the popular psychology, business, and spiritual literature. All of these books and studies point out the personal benefits of using mindfulness practices ("the mind watching the mind"). The difference for those with Affluence Intelligence is that they take action, and *use what they learn from being mindful to move forward toward getting what they want.*

A Willingness to Take Responsibility

Those with Affluence Intelligence take responsibility for what they say and do. They do not place blame for their feelings, thoughts, or actions on others. This does not mean that they always do things perfectly, or that they please everyone at work or at home, but they often gain the respect of others even when they make mistakes. When they are in error, they say they are sorry. They do not get defensive, and they do not deny what they did. They accept their responsibility in what happened, and then they try to do better. They practice the ethos of "the buck stops here." In the words of one of our clients, "I do what I say and say what I do."

We admire those who admit that they did something wrong and take responsibility for it. People with Affluence Intelligence benefit, both psychologically and socially, from taking responsibility and having integrity about their choices. Whether rightly or wrongly, they are seen as being leaders who are not afraid to admit what they have done and own up to it. We commonly say that such a person "has character." But taking responsibility does more than simply demonstrate that you have character: It streamlines, rather than inhibits or stalls, the process of learning and renavigating the course when there is change or conflict. When you take responsibility quickly and without drama, situations are more likely to resolve, and then you can move on.

A Strong Sense of Identity

Having a strong sense of identity—a core sense of who you are, and what defines you as a unique individual—is crucial. We establish a sense of who we are during childhood, and then evolve and refine it throughout our lives. While knowing who they are at any particular point in time, affluent people understand that their sense of self is shaped by dynamic, fluid, evolutionary forces. They could not have unlocked Affluence Intelligence if they insisted on having a sense of self that was static or overly governed by the past.

Through the years of working with people in therapy, we have repeatedly seen that when one holds on to a past identity that is no longer valid, it can disable one's current sense of self. Jessica, a forty-five-year-old client, has had a very strong and powerful identity as a businesswoman. She leads a rich life and has many friends and hobbies. Suddenly she started waking up each morning feeling very empty, and couldn't tell why. After spending an hour with her, we figured it out. Her last child was about to go off to college, and Jessica hadn't realized how much of her identity was linked to her being a mother. When she understood this, her feelings made more sense. She was able to understand the very real changes she was undergoing, and to refocus her direction in life. She joined a group for empty nesters, finding both emotional support and inspiration. She forged a new identity for herself in an area of interest that was close to her heart, working on the board of a national charity helping underserved youth to make life choices that were healthy.

For the truly affluent, a sense of personal value, self-respect, and identity are based on more than wealth. A solid core of self-esteem is created by a multitude of other factors, including the capacity to love and to be loved, to be recognized and connected to family and community, and to be successful and productive. If there is one truth we have learned in working with the very wealthy, it is that a person must develop a strong sense of identity that is not primarily dependent upon his or her bank balance.

Certainly the achievement of financial independence—a symbol of success in our society—can enhance self-esteem. Earned wealth, as the result of great achievement, can be an important building block of a positive self-identity. However, money and professional success by themselves do not usually provide adequate, stable self-esteem. In working with the newly rich, we have come to understand that their achievement of financial success triggered a four-step developmental process we called "Wealth Identity Development."[2] During this process the individual progressively "owns" the ways in which life has changed with money, culminating in a sense of stewardship for oneself, family, and society. In this process we saw how people also needed to get a sense of pleasure from using their money—that is, from the lifestyles they create for themselves, and the beneficial impact their wealth has on others. Yes, there is a fun side to this equation: Those with Affluence Intelligence get a positive and strong sense of identity by enjoying and spending their money. They buy things that are meaningful to them, and they buy things that bring them joy and pleasure. Yet they balance their spending by using their wealth as a resource to bring about positive change—whether within their homes, or in society at large. It is useful to be aware of whether your spending patterns bring together both pleasure and meaning.

How we achieve a strong sense of identity and self-esteem is a slow, changing, evolving dynamic. When we look at the lives of those who have Affluence Intelligence, we see them find an optimal balance of priorities, shifting as they age. They adjust their life strategy to both desired and unexpected change. Unlocking Affluence Intelligence to cultivate a positive and affluent identity requires answering the question that most Americans only dream of having the chance to answer: what is the real meaning and purpose of my money—for me, my family, and my community?

Ambition

Having ambition means wanting to achieve a certain goal. You know what you want and you go after it, without apology. It is that feeling of being driven to go somewhere that you know you want to go, even if you don't have a map or navigational system to get you there. Madonna appeared on *American Bandstand* in the early 1980s and astonished everyone with her song "Like a Virgin." After her performance, when she was asked by Dick Clark what she wanted in her future, she replied, simply, "To rule the world." And she went from living in squalor with no hot water to being one of the most famous and best-selling artists of all time. She could not have done this without ambition. And she didn't try to hide that ambition; she was proud of it.

Ambition is also a way of establishing your position in the world, to demonstrate your unique capacities, and to have a very personal sense of accomplishment. This is particularly important if you have lived in the shadow of a successful parent or other family member. Many of our clients felt burdened by the fame and success of their parents. They wonder if they are expected to reach the same level of achievement or notoriety. They worry that if they follow in a parent's footsteps, will that make whatever they achieve less than that of the successful parent? Jonathan, a fifty-year-old independently successful entrepreneur whose father was a very successful businessman, told us: "One of the greatest gifts my father gave me was not giving me a job. He had a strong antinepotism belief and I was raised knowing that it was against his company policy to hire relatives. I have had such an incredible career and if I had gone to work for my father, I wouldn't have had it. While I'm confident I still would have been successful, I would have always felt the stigma that my father gave me my job, and that I didn't really earn it."

Competitiveness

The affluent love to win. It is not for selfish reasons—it is for the thrill of the chase, and the excitement of seeing who will come out in front. Olympic athletes who go for the gold get a huge rush from trying to beat the competition. And often, if they don't get the gold, they still congratulate the athlete who did. Whether we are talking about a game of cards, the game of business, or the game of celebrity—the affluent love to play it.

Those who have unlocked Affluence Intelligence, who are ambitious and competitive, may appear to be competing against other people, but they are actually competing against themselves. They want to be the very best they can be. Of course, they enjoy doing better than others, but at the end of the day they are challenging themselves, and the vision they have for where they want to go. As Peter said, "I'm very competitive, but far more internally than externally—meaning my focus is more on how well I can do rather than on how I do compared to someone else. I want to do the best I can and am capable of, regardless of what someone else does. I think this is reflected in my primary interest in individual competitive sports versus team sports."

It is a very rare person who has strengths in all Affluence Intelligence behaviors and attitudes. Affluent people, like most of us, have strengths in some areas and vulnerabilities in others. How they approach their strengths and vulnerabilities is different from most people. They are hyper focused on using their strengths, and on finding ways to improve their vulnerabilities. If they can't improve, then they find someone who can handle that area for them. It takes courage to acknowledge your strengths and vulnerabilities, and then to work on using your best capacities to ensure that your vulnerabilities do not get in your way.

chapter five

THE AIQ TEST: EVALUATE YOUR BEHAVIORS AND ATTITUDES

*I*n this second part of the quiz, you will assess your behaviors and attitudes. As we have said, you should not answer questions as you feel you *should* or as you wish you were—answer them as you actually are, even if it is painful to be honest. Give yourself plenty of time to take the quiz carefully and thoughtfully—don't rush through it. As you are responding to the questions, try to come up with a concrete example of when you actually exhibited a certain behavior. For example, you might say, "Yes, I have evidence that I am open-minded. I don't like hardcore motorcycle types. But when my daughter started dating a guy with a Harley and a ton of tattoos,

I decided to get to know him. And it turned out that under all those tattoos, he was a great guy."

To keep yourself honest, you might consider having someone who knows you well look over your answers when you are finished. Or, if you are feeling unsure about how to respond, you might ask friends or loved ones questions like, Have you ever witnessed me suffer a disappointment and then rally and move on? or, Do you think I that am an optimistic person? You may be surprised by the answers you get. Even better, have someone who knows you well take the quiz as if they were you, take it yourself, and then use the average of the scores for each section.

Finally, keep in mind that you are responding about your attitudes and behaviors for both how you are at work and how you are at home, which can be very different. For example, you might be extremely assertive with your colleagues at work but then become a complete milquetoast with your spouse or children when you get home. In this case, you cannot rate yourself on the high end of assertiveness. You will have to take this into account when taking the test and look at the whole picture, not just one aspect of assertiveness.

SCORING FOR PART B, BEHAVIORS AND ATTITUDES

Under each category of behaviors and attitudes there will be a number of statements that you will rate depending on how much you agree or disagree. Assign points per the scale below, and then add up your score in each section.

Answer	Points
I disagree very much	1 point
I disagree moderately	3 points

I disagree slightly	5 points
I agree slightly	6 points
I agree moderately	8 points
I agree very much	10 points

Write the score next to the statement, and then tally your results. Each behavior or attitude has ten questions. Add up all your points and then divide the total score by ten. (If your total score is a fraction, like 87.6, then round up to 88.) Looking across at all eight of your scores, note which are the highest and lowest. These reflect your strengths and the areas that you may want to focus on in the future.

Behaviors

1. RESILIENCE

___ I bounce back quickly from disappointments.

___ I readily learn from my mistakes.

___ I get over my mistakes and move on.

___ When tough things happen, they don't set me back significantly.

___ I can handle the emotions that come with bad or sad news without getting overwhelmed or stuck.

___ I don't make my explanation of what went wrong in a situation my excuse for not moving forward.

___ When challenged, I focus on what is needed to best handle the problem.

___ I find it easy to regain my composure when I am upset or when someone else is upset with me.

___ If I am feeling negative, I can wait and gain perspective about a problem or situation before taking action.

___ I can handle the feelings that come with rejection and still try again.

_____ **Total Resilience:**

2. ASSERTIVENESS

____ If my meal isn't cooked the way I like it, I let the waiter know.

____ If someone says no to me when I ask for something I want, I feel fine asking for it again in a different way.

____ I don't let people interrupt me when I am speaking.

____ Even when I am confused about something or feel stupid not knowing something, I ask questions.

____ I speak up for myself when I feel I am not being treated well.

____ I believe I have the right to express my opinions, thoughts, and feelings.

____ It is more important to stand up for myself than to be concerned about being liked.

____ I ask for clarification when I don't understand what others are saying.

____ I don't mind disagreeing with someone and sharing a completely different opinion.

____ I do not let people with forceful personalities bully or intimidate me.

_____ **Total Assertiveness**

3. INTERPERSONAL EFFECTIVENESS

____ People say that I am very good at understanding their feelings.

____ I am sensitive to the emotional needs of others and can readily empathize with them.

____ When I am in a particular mood, I can recognize what that mood is about and share that with others.

____ I am strongly attuned to my own feelings.

____ People seek me out to help with their emotional concerns.

____ I can shake off my negative feelings in service of a team effort or common goal.

___ I believe that collaboration is the key to success.

___ I am aware of body language or other social signals that show the feelings or needs of others.

___ I have the skills and strategies necessary to resolve my conflicts with others.

___ When I am upset, I am still able to communicate my feelings clearly, and to hear about those of others.

_____ **Total Interpersonal Effectiveness**

4. ABILITY TO WORK HARD AND ACHIEVE GOALS

___ I am able to motivate myself to try and try again in the face of setbacks.

___ When I want something, I do everything possible to get it.

___ I don't let distractions get in the way of my goal.

___ I can focus and follow through on my goals even when I have to give up enjoyable activities I might otherwise be doing.

___ I work hard to get what I want.

___ When I face an obstacle, I find a way to keep going, even when others would give up.

___ Others see me as very goal oriented.

___ Others see me as driven to get what I want.

___ I keep a "to-do" list and get through the majority of it daily.

___ I never quit before I complete a task I have set my mind to accomplish.

_____ **Total Ability to Work Hard and Achieve Goals**

Attitudes

5. OPTIMISM

___ I often see possibilities where others do not.

___ I like to give people the benefit of the doubt.

___ I most often think that things will work out all right.

___ I see the cup as more than half full.

___ I don't have time for naysayers.

___ I believe that I can make good things happen.

___ I believe that I can get what I want—and if I don't, then I believe I'll soon find something as good or better.

___ I often feel lucky.

___ Even when I have a bad day, I always know tomorrow may be better.

___ I see problems as temporary obstacles that I believe I can overcome.

_____ **Total Optimism**

6. OPEN-MINDEDNESS AND CURIOSITY

___ I am always interested in learning why people think and feel the way they do, even when I disagree with them.

___ I can usually look at a situation and see the differing points of view.

___ I am a true life-long learner.

___ People say that I ask a lot of questions.

___ People often say they do not feel judged by me.

___ I am always curious to learn about the diverse experiences, knowledge, and beliefs of other people.

___ I can help solve problems by thinking outside the box.

___ I like to try new things to find out if I will like them.

___ I face new situations with an open mind.

___ I learn from my experiences and from the experiences of others.

_____ **Total Open-mindedness and Curiosity**

7. A SENSE OF CONTROL OVER ONE'S LIFE

___ I take responsibility for my part in most situations.

___ When others do not like me, I don't feel compelled to be "overly nice" or compliant so that they will start to like me more.

___ After something has upset me, I can readily regain my composure.

___ My belief in myself gets me through difficult times.

___ I am comfortable taking a stand on something, even in the face of strong opposition.

___ I have a consistent sense of who I am as a person, regardless of where I am or who I am with.

___ I see myself as being in command of my life.

___ I am responsible for my moods, good or bad.

___ I have the ability to pause and reflect before I act.

____ **Total Sense of Control Over Your Life**

8. AMBITION

___ Others say that I'm very focused and goal oriented.

___ I am clear on my goals, in life and at work.

___ I know what I want and I go for it.

___ I thrive on competing for a desired outcome.

___ Others tell me that I am driven.

___ I love to compete and I love to win.

___ I'll do whatever it takes to achieve my goals.

___ I love setting goals for work or play.

___ I get up every day looking forward to working my list of goals.

___ People say that I both work and play very hard.

____ **Total Ambition**

YOUR SCORES FOR PART B

Behaviors & Attitudes	Scores
1. Resilience	_____
2. Assertiveness	_____
3. Interpersonal effectiveness	_____
4. Ability to work hard	_____
5. Optimism	_____
6. Open mindedness	_____
7. Sense of control of one's life	_____
8. Ambition	_____
TOTAL PART B SCORE:	_____

(Transfer this score to page 154,
so you can obtain your total AIQ score).

chapter six

RAISING YOUR PERSONAL DOW: BECOMING FINANCIALLY EFFECTIVE

*A*re you living in a "money fog?" Many of us seem to lack a clear understanding of our money dynamics—how much is coming in, or how much is going out, and what we need for our future security. Some of us would rather not think about money at all, because doing so creates initial discomfort. But living in a fog leaves us stagnant, uncertain, directionless, fearful, and vulnerable to losing our hard-earned cash.

In contrast, people who are financially effective are both competent and secure in their relationship with money. We see this as having the capacities of both *financial competency* and *financial ease*. They know the importance of having a money plan, have gained financial literacy, and have found their comfort zone with money. If you want to raise your personal Dow, you will need to raise your financial effectiveness.

Financial competency is about having a money plan and understanding the mechanics of money management. Think of your money as flowing in and out of five buckets: earning, spending, saving, investing, and sharing. A money plan with Affluence Intelligence is based on operating values that you have determined for each of these buckets. Your values should reflect careful thought in which you determine what is a financial *need* and what is a financial *want*. The plan will then include rules and guidelines for how you will live your values, for how money will go in and out of each of five buckets. For example, if you value "living within my means," then your plan would have rules about not spending outside of what you can afford, which may include limitations on use of credit cards and loans. If you value "long-term financial security," then your plan would include putting aside a percentage of your earnings into savings or investments. (You can get this process started by doing the three-month AI plan outlined later in this book.) Knowing the basics of the marketplace and of money management will give you the core information and tools to help you strategize the most efficient and effective ways to get what you want for yourself.

These basics will help you to assess your needs and your wants, and help you determine the financial plan that will best meet your desired goals. Don't worry, we're not saying you have to become an accountant or a math wiz. But it does mean taking the time and having the self-discipline to improve your financial literacy, and to develop a financial plan that is attuned to your core values. Just as you would take care of a prized possession, such as a sports car, a photo album from your childhood, or a favorite piece of artwork, so too should you take care of your money. Like most of our clients, you can get help with your financial life by using the services of financial planners, accountants, and financial consultants. You may also choose to get help from a trusted friend who is financially savvy. Even when you have help, a person who has financial competency stays keenly aware and in charge of his or her earning, saving, investing, spending, and sharing of money. Oprah Winfrey, one of the wealthiest women on the planet, has said that it is vital that she herself signs every single check that goes out of her company. She wants to know exactly what is happening to her money.

Managing your money uses simple concepts that do not require more than basic math skills typically learned in high school. Having a money plan, and being conversant in the language of finances, is crucial to achieving financial success.

Raising your "personal Dow"—become financially effective. As we described in Chapter 1, when you raise your financial effectiveness quotient, you raise your likelihood of feeling both in charge of, and at ease with, the way you earn, spend, save, invest, and share your money. It starts with knowing the financial basics. What does it take for you (and your life partner) to be financially secure and responsible?

- Take control of your money. Get organized, think about your money in five buckets:
  › Earning
  › Spending
  › Saving
  › Investing
  › Sharing

- Gain comfort and ease in talking about money.
- Learn and understand banking and financial marketplace basics.
- Determine your core money values about:
  › Earning
  › Spending
  › Saving
  › Investing
  › Sharing
- Create a budget for your daily life needs and wants:
  › Divide your assets among each of the five buckets, as possible
  › Affluence Intelligence Key: Live within your means.
- Build a short- and long-term financial plan that is aligned with your core values, and that fits with your age and level of responsibility. Determine your
  › financial goals, short and long term
  › your risk tolerance to guide your investment strategy
  › how much to budget for insurance, and to have an emergency backup fund
  › big ticket saving needs: College, retirement, health care
- Determine benchmarks for earning, investing, saving, spending, and sharing of money.
- Find the professional help you need to implement your plan (financial advisor, planner, accountant, attorney).
- Be accountable. Track your progress on a written chart. Involve a friend or advisor to keep you on track and honest!

So people with financial competency know what they bring home every month, have a plan for saving, and have a clear sense of what they can spend without undermining their financial plan. Their charitable giving, regardless of the amount, is part of the plan. They take care to make financial decisions that are in accordance with their level of risk tolerance. While not necessarily financial experts, they take charge of their financial decision making. They understand how to read a balance sheet, and can understand their annual 1040 tax return.

The second part of financial effectiveness is about reaching a personal comfort zone with money. We call this having "financial ease." When you have this capacity, then money does not cause you insecurity, anxiety, guilt, embarrassment, or shame. You have attained psychological comfort with how you think and feel about the earning, saving, spending, and sharing of money, regardless of the size of your portfolio. Money is not the sole motivator for what you do, nor does it define who you are. Rather, money is seen as a tool and as a resource in your life, not overdetermining your self-esteem or sense of personal meaning or happiness. You have financial ease when you feel a sense of control of your money, rather than money controlling you. Look at Howard's life—he wasn't wealthy in the Bill Gates sense of the term, but he had attained a sufficient degree of emotional and financial well-being about his money. When you have financial ease, you are better equipped to handle the interplay of money matters and life issues, such as your love relationships, career challenges, and raising children. At its best, financial ease allows you to take care of your needs and to use money as a tool to enjoy, to feel secure, to be generous, and to do things that are important to you.

Then there are people like David the architect who make lots of money, and even have a substantial retirement fund, but do not feel at peace and secure with their relationship to money. David's story, echoed by many of our far wealthier clients, has shown us how financial ease will never be attained by simply having more money. Nor does your level of financial education automatically provide you with the security and peace that comes with financial ease. In fact, having more money may lead you to feel a great deal of anxiety and uncertainty. We coined the phrase "Sudden Wealth Syndrome" to describe the psychological experience of a person without money who suddenly comes into a lot of it, finding that their lack of financial ease leads them to actually feeling more vulnerable and insecure. That's the interesting part of Sudden Wealth Syndrome: If money was an end point, then people wouldn't have these problems. But in fact the distress or impairment that people experience as a consequence of sudden wealth is in excess of what one would ordinarily expect.

People with financial ease feel empowered in their relationship to money: They can make the necessary and sometimes difficult lifestyle choices in order to gain or maintain their security and peace. When money problems arise, they take leadership in answering the call. So when Jack, a thirty-eight-year-old contractor, lost his full-time job and only could find part-time work, he figured out how to reduce his debt—which meant moving from a house to an apartment, and curtailing his leisure spending, so that he could reduce the stress of having less money. Of course, many of us cannot completely reduce our debt load, given the commitments we have made, or even necessarily find alternative employment, especially when unemployment is at a high rate. Nevertheless, people with financial ease feel empowered to make money decisions in order to take actions that recalibrate to their changing financial circumstances. We've seen some interesting examples of this: Raj, a sixty-five-year-old ex-teacher, has lived outside of the United States for more than a decade, in countries with a much lower cost of living. As he said, "I've become an expert on how to live a happy and inexpensive lifestyle. I don't want to incur any expense that gets in the way of doing what I truly enjoy. I stay away from any spending that will spoil my internal ease." Raj is not one of our wealthy inheritors: He and his wife live off of their social security checks and the occasional part-time job.

FINANCIAL EFFECTIVENESS AND
YOUR MONEY PSYCHOLOGY

While it may seem easy to appreciate the common sense benefits of attaining financial effectiveness, we also understand that for many, becoming financially effective is an elusive and frustrating goal. Unfortunately, the American educational system, for the most part, does not require any curriculum on the fundamentals of the economic system, or financial basics like creating a budget or understanding stocks, bonds, interest rates, alternative investments, and so on. Further, women, even in today's world, are still subject to a second-class status about money matters. Even in top-paying jobs they still make on average less money (10–20 percent less, depending on the type of job) than men.[1]

This includes professional careers, such as medicine, in which female physicians make significantly less money than their male counterparts.[2] While women have made great strides in leadership in the corporate and political world, they still face barriers.

When many of us have conversations with friends or with family about money, we find that money is a lightning rod, charged with strong feelings, fantasies, religious beliefs, cultural associations, and poignant family stories of great joy and loss. We have been repeatedly struck by the simple fact that it is very hard for people to simply think about or have a conversation about money that is just about money; inevitably other feelings and issues colonize the discussion. Like the topic of sex fifty years ago, many of us would just as soon avoid the shock waves of facing our feelings and attitudes about money. Yet ignorance does not bring bliss, but rather

a continuation of the same frustrations and sense of disempower-
ment that get in the way of unlocking your Affluence Intelligence.

To master this challenge and increase your AI, we need to un-
pack the feelings, beliefs, and attitudes that comprise your money
psychology. Indeed, each of us has a unique psychology about the
saving, spending, sharing, and investing of money that has been
shaped by forces within ourselves—our very own personal history
with money. These forces work together to provide the code for our
psychological software about money. How we think, feel, and behave in regard to money—our personal programs that determine
how we spend, invest, save, or share it, all reflect our individual
money psychology. The more you know about your money psychology, the more empowered you are to revise, update, or change
your personal software that drives (or stalls) your decision making.

Unfortunately, we make many important financial decisions
based on our money psychology software, which operates in the
background, often out of our direct awareness, in the form of
deeply held values and beliefs. Some of these values fit well with
the real money issues of our current lives, while other values are
the remnants of the past that have become irrelevant or obsolete.
Gaining clarity on the values that drive your financial decision
making is key to attaining financial effectiveness and unlocking
your Affluence Intelligence. For example, Paul called us with an
interesting dilemma. His father had just passed away and left him
a fortune. He wanted to get rid of it as fast as he could because, as
he said, "Dad was not a good man. This money was made exploiting
many others; he used them and threw them away. Dad was a leader
in globalization of the workforce. His company had markedly increased its earnings by replacing many long-term employees with
lower paid workers overseas. Dad was focused on the bottom line,
not paying attention to the pain caused by his actions. When I confronted him with the pain he had caused for many of these em-

ployees' families that we knew for years, he just ignored me or changed the subject. I was so disappointed in him, and so alienated by his actions, that I grew distant."

Paul had heard from his financial advisor that MMCI worked with psychological and ethical issues of the suddenly wealthy. He reached out to us saying, "I want to handle this the right way." He knew that his leftover feelings about his father were getting in the way of taking a reasoned approach to his situation. Paul did not want to repeat his father's money values or actions, but was not clear about what he should do. He had never really thought through his own money values, nor had he considered the opportunities that this new inheritance afforded him. We helped him think through and develop a set of money values relevant to his current situation. We also helped him consider ways in which he could use this inheritance as a resource for making a difference. Gaining clarity on money values (which you can do for yourself by using the AI method in this book) enabled Paul to see that what he did with his inheritance did not have to mimic his father's values or actions, but rather his own. He reset his AI thermostat to feel empowered rather than burdened by this inheritance. For example, he chose to use some of it to support organizations involved in worker's rights, and to support programs offering vocational training of those whose jobs in manufacturing had become obsolete. For Paul, these charitable gifts were acts of redemption, an expression of his desire to heal some of the damage done by his father's company in the wealth accumulation process.[3]

DISCOVERING YOUR MONEY PSYCHOLOGY: SCARCITY AND ABUNDANCE

Our values about money live above and below the surface of everyday awareness.

You may, for example, see yourself as a "giving" person, but find that you harbor fears about ever having enough money to feel truly secure. Discovering your money psychology means understanding how both the overt and hidden forces influence your money values. In this vein, we should never underestimate how our family background, culture, and religion influence whether we see finances as a world of scarce resources or a world where there will always be plenty. Think of deeply held beliefs about scarcity and abundance on a psychological continuum. Some of us carry beliefs that sit closer to the scarcity end, while others have attitudes and beliefs that reflect endless abundance. We have seen the risks at both ends. For example, we have seen how a family history of financial scarcity or loss can disrupt financial ease even in cases of individuals who have accumulated great wealth. We have worked with some very wealthy people who had what we call "bag lady syndrome"—in which a person who is a multimillionaire can never attain financial ease, for they live constantly in fear of waking up tomorrow to having nothing. These irrational fears are frequently the carryover from parents or grandparents who struggled through the Great Depression, the Holocaust, or a history of family members who gambled money away. Consequentially, those with bag lady syndrome are perennially insecure about money, anticipating the catastrophe that is just around the corner.

At the other end of the scarcity-abundance continuum are those people who are deluded by irrational exuberance, who seem to believe that money will show up no matter how much they are in debt. They are the recipients of family money messages that essentially say, "Don't worry, no matter how much you mess up, you will always be taken care of." This may be the legacy of the overly protective spouse, father, or friend. Some seem to make life choices that inevitably lead, over and over, to financial crisis and bail-out—

in which they repeatedly engage in problematic situations that require the need for a financial rescue. They can go to the very edge of their finances, because of their deeply held belief that if they fail, they will be rescued.

Think about where you stand on this continuum. Become aware of the family and cultural messages that cultivate your feelings and thoughts about scarcity and abundance. Do these beliefs still fit with who you are today, or where you want to go in life? What are the values that make sense for you, that will increase your AI thermostat?

MONEY ANXIETY

Many of us are very smart about most matters, but have "a thing" about money. When it comes to financial matters, it seems we are being controlled by inner voices that make us feel helpless and stupid. Listen to Joelle's story: She was a competent professor of history who was masterful with the details of her work, yet couldn't handle the basics of financial planning. Even reading her monthly statements made her anxious and overwhelmed. She solved her anxiety by not opening the statements. Joelle came from a successful business family in which the lineage of succession always excluded the daughters. She was expected to be a good wife and mother and to find a career that would be socially useful. In her family, girls were not included in any financial conversations or business discussions. Consequently, as her boyfriend said, "You are funny about money." She carried her family's deeply held values that femininity and financial competence do not work together. While her family supported her academic achievements, their negative money messages impacted her ability to attain financial effectiveness. Even though Joelle clearly had the intelligence to be financially effective, her money psychology, albeit unconscious, set her baseline with the belief that financial competence was an act of disloyalty to her family's core values.

SPENDERS AND SAVERS

Your money psychology is also reflected in your attitudes and beliefs about the spending and saving of money. Sometimes it seems that the world is divided between people who came out of the womb as either spenders or savers. Spenders take pleasure in spending. For them, money is to be enjoyed, and financial risks are worth taking. Being generous, giving to others and to charity feels great. Retail therapy is satisfying. Savers take pleasure in saving, sometimes to the extreme of hoarding. They feel more secure and happy as their bank accounts grow. They are more risk averse. They are very careful about what they give and what they promise. Interestingly, spenders and savers often end up marrying each other, expressing an unconscious wish for one's partner to help balance one's natural tendencies about money. Unfortunately, this desire for balance is usually undermined by the psychological tendency to repeat what is familiar, to reinforce our patterns, for better or worse. So instead of creating a mutually beneficial collaboration, spenders and savers end up on a collision course, each partner fighting to ensure that his or her voice is heard.

TAKING RESPONSIBILITY
FOR YOUR MONEY PSYCHOLOGY

You may lean toward being a spender or saver, and have a better appreciation of your attitudes about scarcity versus abundance. Bottom line, you need to use this awareness to take personal responsibility for becoming financially effective, to attain both financial ease and financial competency. Don't fall into the trap of blaming your partner, your parents, or the world for your own financial ineffectiveness. And don't form agreements in which your partner's lack of financial effectiveness can drown you. Keep your eyes wide open and keep in touch with the financial matters of your relationship, no matter how good it may look on the surface. We have seen so many people who lived at the edge of their financial capacity before the Great Recession. They attained financial ease by telling themselves the false story that the economy will only get better. Then one of the two partners loses a job, then a car, then they can't make their overly leveraged mortgage payments, and in less than a year, they have lost not only financial ease, but the very backbone of their lives.

To be financially effective, financial ease and financial competency must work in concert, and be part of a plan that takes into account the changes and challenges of adult development. We've seen many people who have financial ease in the short term, only to find that they lack a navigator for their later years. Financial ease can be readily undermined by vulnerabilities in financial competency. For example, Cindy was a successful dance teacher and performer whose life focused on dance, not money. In her twenties and thirties she earned enough to live a frugal lifestyle that made dance the focus. She didn't worry about money, and she was happy. Then at forty, her body started to show signs of wear. She couldn't work as long or as hard. She had to face the fact that she did not plan for her own future personal and financial security. Now she is up to her ears in debt, struggling with money anxieties. This story is similar to many of the baby boomers who, from a financial perspective, lived for today and then found themselves worrying about tomorrow.[4]

At its core, being financially effective—having financial ease and financial competency—means that you have a solid hold on your finances, characterized by the feeling of truly "owning your money." Unlocking this part of your Affluence Intelligence means having a financial awakening. The challenge is to stay awake and take action. Unfortunately, most of us take a look and go back into the fog. If you put this part of your AI off, or pretend you just can't understand math, or tell yourself the false story of how you can never feel comfortable with money, then we can promise that you will never unlock your Affluence Intelligence. The hard work is challenging your own story of why you can't. This means doing a review of the money messages, sorting out the ways in which you protect yourself from change, and determining your personal money values. The first step is to say, "Yes." The next step is to do our three-month program and make use of the wealth of resources readily available on this topic.[5]

chapter seven

THE AIQ TEST: EVALUATE YOUR FINANCIAL EFFECTIVENESS

SCORING FOR PART C: FINANCIAL EFFECTIVENESS

Under each category of financial effectiveness (financial competency and financial ease) there will be a number of statements that you will rate depending on how much you agree or disagree. Assign points per the scale below, and then add up your score in each section.

Answer	Points
I disagree very much	1 point
I disagree moderately	3 points

I disagree slightly	5 points
I agree slightly	6 points
I agree moderately	8 points
I agree very much	10 points

Write the score next to the statement, and then tally your results. Each category has ten questions. Add up all your points and then divide the total score by ten. (If your total score is a fraction, like 18.6, then round up to 19.) Looking at all eight of your scores, note which are the highest and lowest. These reflect your strengths and the areas that you want to focus on in the future.

FINANCIAL EFFECTIVENESS

FINANCIAL COMPETENCY

___ I have a budget that I follow.

___ I live within my means.

___ I have a backup emergency fund for myself and my family.

___ I look at my bank statements and balance my checkbook every month.

___ I read and understand my credit card statements.

___ I am saving for my retirement.

___ I have a plan for the saving, spending, and sharing of my money.

___ I understand the basics of the American marketplace: stocks, bonds, private equity investments, mutual funds, and so on.

___ I always know how much money I have.

___ I have enough money for my needs and wants.

_____ **Total Financial Competency**

FINANCIAL EASE

___ I make money decisions by careful analysis rather than by impulse.

___ My financial status does not cause me shame or embarrassment or guilt.

___ How much money I have does not determine my self-esteem.

___ I am free and comfortable to do what I want with my money.

___ My sense of personal power is not affected by the amount of money I have.

___ I have the right to make financial decisions in my own home.

___ I am comfortable having conversations about money matters in my close relationships.

___ Money is not the primary motivator of my most important life decisions.

___ I feel comfortable with myself even when I'm with people who have much more money than I do.

___ When I'm with a person who has nicer things than I do (jewelry, home, car), I don't feel inferior or overly envious.

_____ **Total Financial Ease**

YOUR SCORES FOR PART C

Financial Effectiveness	*Scores*
1. Financial Competency	_____
2. Financial Ease	_____
TOTAL PART C SCORE:	_____

(Transfer this score to page 154, so you can obtain your total AIQ score).

chapter eight

RESETTING YOUR AI THERMOSTAT: MANAGING OBSTACLES THAT GET IN YOUR WAY

YOUR AFFLUENCE INTELLIGENCE BASELINE: UNDERSTANDING HOW YOUR THERMOSTAT WORKS

It would be great if you could simply decide to change whatever you wanted and increase your AIQ. But we're not built that way. Each of us has an inner regulatory mechanism that establishes a baseline for AI. This baseline is what you feel is normal, given your psychology, personal history, and cultural background. This regulatory system, like the autonomic body systems, acts outside of your direct awareness to keep you functioning at a certain level. This level may feel "normal," but may set your AIQ too low. Ultimately, your baseline affects your AIQ, which then determines your attainment level on the seven factors of AIQ. Psychologists say that we all have what they call a "happiness set point." A study once showed that people who had been disabled in bad accidents were often angry and depressed directly afterwards. But within eighteen months, they went back to the level of happiness they had before the accident. Those who were naturally happy people went back to being basically happy, and those who were not happy before went back to where they had been as well. For example, your inner regulator may overdetermine how much money you feel comfortable with, or how much joy you will have in relationships, or how much you will love your work. So to change your AIQ, you need to understand the ways in which your inner regulatory system gets in your way or sets your expectations too low. Our program provides you with the tools to make the changes necessary to really get what you want.

Think of your regulatory system operating like the thermostat in your home. Let's say you set it at 74 degrees. If it gets too cold, the heater kicks on and warms up the house. If it gets too hot, the air conditioning comes on and cools the place down. Because of how your thermostat is set, you can maintain a comfortable temperature in your home at any given time, no matter what's going on outside—whether there is a heat wave or an arctic blast.

If you have a high thermostatic setting (you have healthy self-esteem, financial effectiveness, and feel you deserve wealth) and you lose your money, you will find a way to recoup your losses. If you have a low setting (you have low self-esteem, vulnerability in financial effectiveness, and lack a healthy sense of entitlement), you will find ways (often unconsciously) to lose your money until you return to a level that feels normal for you—your inner regulator has returned you to your baseline. The problem is that your normal baseline may not actually be sufficient, especially if you are not earning enough to cover your needs and wants. "Normal" is simply what is familiar and predictable, even if it actually makes you unhappy, stressed out, and in debt. If your baseline normal is set low, then you cannot "trust your gut instincts," which may pull you down into your non-affluent comfort zone.

It's not just money that you can lose—if your affluence thermostat is set too low, you may find ways to get rid of other things that make you happy (such as a loving marriage) to get back to what is familiar (being alone), even while telling others, such as a therapist (and truly believing yourself), that you don't want the marriage to end.

The fact is that change can be scary, even when that change is for the better. Let's take as an example our client Dennis, who won the lottery. He was suddenly in a situation that was totally unfamiliar to him, and much to his surprise it did not make him happy. He was not used to having all that wealth, and it made him feel less than enough, because he felt he now had to do something world-changing with his money. He also felt as though he had no direction in his life. So instead of being overjoyed with his new millionaire status, he started feeling anxious and depressed. He started to travel extensively just to get away from the pressure he felt being around people who knew him before he had money.

In his work with us, he shared a crucial event that made him see his life differently. His grandmother had recently passed away. After the funeral, he came to us and said, "You know, she was such a simple woman, and she loved life. And I'm a simple person, too. I'm coming back to myself—I'm starting to be happy again because I have gone back to doing the simple things that I love, such as playing soccer, volunteering at a local school, or seeing family and friends. I no longer feel I have to solve the world's problems just because I have all this money."

His story, showing how people deal with their discomfort over money, is key: they either take action to raise the setting on their thermostat (a healthy reaction), or they unwittingly lower their financial temperature by blowing through the money (an unhealthy reaction). Fortunately, Dennis was able to think about his relationship with his money in a new way—a way that he could live with comfortably. He raised the setting on his thermostat.

Your thermostat is set by a number of different factors, many of which are rooted in childhood experience. For example, if you were taught that money is power and you do not feel comfortable having power, your thermostat will be set low. Perhaps you are like Pamela, an administrative assistant who complains about the stresses of living paycheck to paycheck and says that she wants something more. However, she feels very comfortable living the routine of her daily life. Her friends, her activities, her lifestyle struggles—even what she complains about—feel like a pair of comfortable old shoes. She says she wants to raise her Affluence Intelligence thermostat, but does nothing about it because she subconsciously fears that if she raises her thermostat, she will lose what she has. Having grown up in a working class Brooklyn family with four siblings who neither moved out nor up in social class, she was used to her thermostat being set low. Living this familiar lifestyle may have its limitations, but if it is your life, you may be unwilling to discard it for an unknown new one, particularly when your parents, siblings, and friends are all living the same lifestyle.

Luckily, you can transcend the fears and childhood messages that keep your Affluence Intelligence thermostat set at the low end. Those with Affluence Intelligence have learned how to manage the impact of the past. Now you can learn how to do it, too—by determining your AIQ, and then by making conscious changes.

As far as we are concerned, there is no good or bad when it comes to where you set your thermostat, as long as it is serving you well. However, because you are reading this book, chances are that you feel your thermostat is set too low. The good news is that by changing your thermostat you can unlock your Affluence Intelligence. It can take some effort to make that change because the ways we behave are often so unconscious. For example, Alex wanted to earn more, but somehow never could. When we talked to him about his childhood, he told us that his father had worked in a tool manufacturing factory all his life. Like Pamela who couldn't betray her working class roots, on some deeply unconscious level, Alex felt it would be disloyal and disrespectful to make more money than his father ever had.

To get a sense of your thermostat setting about money, it can be an interesting exercise to run some numbers in your mind. How would you feel making $40,000 a year? $75,000? What about $150,000? What about $250,000? (Keep upping the numbers by just 100s if need be.) At some point, your thermostat will kick in and you will start to feel discomfort. Finding out why can be a key to raising your Affluence Intelligence thermostat because it is possible to get used to earning more at almost any stage of life.

Those with Affluence Intelligence do not feel this kind of discomfort around money—or if they do, they quickly get over it. Those who created wealth generally have a sense of pride about it. They say, I worked hard for this, and I deserve it. This is not hubris; they just feel that they have earned it. They are excited and feel blessed and lucky—and, most importantly, they are comfortable with their wealth. In our experience, these people are driven by achievement, not simply by money. Money is a happy by-product of their achievement and the benefit of being successful.

Raising your thermostat means creating change in your life, and as we have said, change can cause discomfort. Sometimes you have to feel worse (moving away from the familiar) before you feel better (having more affluence). But the short-term discomfort is always worth the long-term gain.

You can tell if you need to raise your thermostat if you are experiencing any anxiety or depression in your life, particularly concerning your attainment on any of the seven factors that comprise Affluence Intelligence. By raising your thermostat, you will have more of our seven factors of affluence.

WHAT IS KEEPING YOUR AFFLUENCE INTELLIGENCE THERMOSTAT SET ON LOW?

Your thermostat setting is directly linked to your psychological defenses, and specifically how they are working for or against you. Beneath the surface, we all have psychological defenses that get in the way of learning and change. Defenses are the ways we protect ourselves from real or imagined stress and strain. They are important coping mechanisms and are necessary to our psychic equilibrium. But they can also become psychological traps that hold us back and keep us stuck—without our realizing it. Defenses can make us feel better for the moment, or help us adapt to a stressful situation, but they can also limit our choices and possibilities. Some defenses may alter our perception of what is or isn't possible. Think of psychological defenses as glasses with different levels of shading we use to protect against what we perceive to be harmful. At times the lens may be too dark to see clearly or we may hide behind them in order not to see clearly. However, there are times when defenses like rationalization, denial, or avoidance, or even the more distorting defenses like "splitting" (that is, all or nothing thinking and/or feeling) actually serve an important function (although you would think they wouldn't), because they can protect the mind when it can't handle reality, at least for the short term.

People who are unaware of their defenses may create beliefs that support them, developing a rationale that provides "the reasons" for why we can or can't think differently, or change an attitude or a behavior. They are more likely to find that their growth and chances of success are limited. Why is this? Perhaps they have not had the right role models or opportunities in life. Or they may not have been educated on how to learn and develop certain attitudes and behaviors, and how to overcome others.

Defenses are a part of daily life. But when people with Affluence Intelligence get tripped up by their defenses, they do not use them as excuses, particularly as to why they don't have more money. Instead, they learn how they can best manage themselves to get what they want. They understand their defenses, and can be flexible in their use.

People who have not unlocked Affluence Intelligence may run up against their defenses when they start thinking about changing their AI baseline. Unfortunately these defenses may be forms of self-protection that provide a sense of safety and predictability, but at a very high price—impeding the ability to reset their Affluence Intelligence thermostat.

Common Beliefs and Defenses

Here are some of the most common beliefs and defenses (often intertwined) that get in the way of resetting your Affluence Intelligence thermostat:

Telling Yourself a False Story

We all tell ourselves stories about who we are and where we have come from. You might tell yourself that you are a victim, that you are a martyr, that you are overburdened, or that you are over-worked. Or that you are too busy to take care of yourself, too smart to learn from others, or somehow more special and more deserving than others. This is a form of self-talk that is not only negative and potentially self-destructive, but more importantly, these stories can undermine your moving forward, and having a life reflects what you say you truly want for yourself. We once counseled a woman named Debra who was in her mid-thirties. She had a lot of energy and had the capacity to make things happen in her professional life. Unfortunately, she had the repeated pattern of earning a large amount of money, and then losing it. This had happened to her at least twice in her life: She had made millions, and then lost it all.

Debra told Stephen, "I come from a family where there was a lot of coming and going, and there was no stability. My father had an affair, which threatened to break up the family. My childhood was riddled with uncertainly about what was going to happen next." The basis for the story that she told herself—that life was always changing and uncertain—was true, but it didn't offer Debra much useful information as to why she undermined herself and always lost what she had. She needed to see that her belief that life was turbulent was driving her behavior in the present. To her surprise, she learned that it was uncomfortable for her to be comfortable and have a stable life. A lifestyle of cyclical chaos felt more familiar. (She once said, "Yes, I'm the queen of the money roller coaster.") Knowing this, she still didn't use what she had learned about herself to get ahead or find a solution to the problem of consistently losing her money.

When Stephen told her that her false story was getting in her way of making changes, her first response was, "You just don't believe that I had a horrible childhood."

He said, "I do believe it. I am just questioning how you are using or not using this information to help your current situation." Eventually he was able to get her to see how much the story was limiting her success, that she was paying a very high price for it, and that life did not necessarily have to be so turbulent. She had to believe it was possible, and that she was entitled, to have a life in which she could be successful and safe.

A false story does not mean that what people think happened to them did not actually happen to them. By repeatedly telling themselves a story about the past as if it is true in the present, they limit their sense of possibility or give themselves an excuse as to why they are not living up to their full potential or capacity. This kind of thinking is a trap that one can fall into all too easily, and is an unhealthy way of coping with real or perceived stress.

When it comes to money and finances, people have many types of stories they use to explain why they are not affluent. They say, in essence, I have failed and here is why. They take a partial truth, make it the whole truth, and then define themselves by it. Or they use a life story as the absolute predictor of the future. It doesn't have to be that way.

Understanding yourself is good. Unfortunately, a focus on understanding can also become a means by which we overidentify with our problems, and build false images of ourselves as chronically inhibited or crippled. This does not lead to affluence—it leads to self-limiting thinking.

Spacing Out
"Spacing out," or dissociation, is a version of the psychological defense of repression. It occurs when we take something that causes us anxiety and put it out of our conscious mind into a kind of psychological storage bank until we feel able to deal with it. When we

put away whatever is causing us discomfort, we are able to forget about it, at least temporarily.

Most of us experience this form of self-protection in our daily lives. Perhaps as you are reading this book you found yourself drifting away into a daydream. Or perhaps at work you lose yourself in a computer game or in a fantasy about going to the movies that night rather than doing your job. These types of defenses give you a little break from your current reality to take some time off from whatever is bothering (or boring) you, so you can feel nurtured and/or excited. Like most defenses, it is very helpful when it does not derail you for any length of time. It becomes a problem if you space out or daydream at the expense of doing your job or the things that are important to you. It becomes a real problem particularly when it comes to money, if you "forget" to do the things that would help you better manage—and expand—your financial portfolio.

Often people may feel stupid when they realize they did not check their credit card statements or balance their bank accounts (and therefore did not catch mistakes that cost them money). But know that the defensive use of spacing out has nothing to do with intelligence.

Spacing out also has nothing to do with memory. Frances is smart, responsible, capable, and has a good memory. If she has to make a phone call, attend a meeting, or pick something up at the grocery store, she will remember to do so. But she often "forgets" to invoice clients for work she has done for them. Because she was told as a child that women should not concern themselves with money, Frances gets very anxious about financial matters. She unconsciously tries to alleviate this anxiety by spacing out and living in her version of "money fog."

Frances is not alone in her behavior. Many people do it; spacing out is one of the most widespread of the healthy defenses, particularly when it comes to money matters. Common examples of people who space out include: the man who plans to ask his boss for a raise but then forgets (he believes) because an urgent project takes his attention, or the woman who forgets to roll over her 401(k) over when she gets a new job.

Social and Cultural Pressures to Conform

Social pressures to live in a certain way are very strong. Too many of us base our financial decisions on what we perceive to be a community standard in order to feel acceptance, or simply to feel good about ourselves. This so-called keeping up with the Joneses creates the pressure to be in style, to be cool, to be seen with the right people in the right places. Examples of this behavior are getting a new dress for an occasion (although you already have a closet full of fine clothes) or getting the latest smartphone (although you won't use most of its features). It can include spending a lot of time and money to make sure you are invited to the right parties and belong to the right clubs and organizations. This can be time and money well spent, as it may be pleasurable, or provide you with social networking opportunities that you can actually use to get where you want to go. But all too often the pressure to "keep up" is simply time and money wasted that are not aligned with your core values or connected to any real action that will take you toward your goal. To the outside world, you look like you are doing well, but if you live beyond your means in order to keep up appearances, you may find yourself up to your eyeballs in debt. Remember David the architect? He and his wife felt the pressure to "keep up," and it resulted in them living beyond their means, and feeling that no matter how hard David worked, nothing was ever enough.

Magical Thinking and Fantasy

The truly affluent take hold of their lives, taking active responsibility for what they do. In contrast, some people hope that change will happen by itself, a belief informed by the magical thinking of the child who lives within each of us, who is waiting for the perfect parent to fix what is wrong or missing, for the White Knight to arrive and save the day, or for wishes to come true simply because we have said them out loud. Having Affluence Intelligence requires facing the fact that childhood, the past, and fantasies about it are over—and that you are now an adult who is in charge of your own life.

The classic example is the man who always has a dream that he never reaches (such as, One day I will be a famous novelist). This is *puer aeternus,* sometimes called the Peter Pan syndrome. There is a fantasy that some day things will be better, without any facts to support this dream (such as if no agent will agree to represent his novel). Magical thinking is also seen in the business world when people fill out sales or performance projection sheets. The sheets look great, on the surface—but writing down what you would like to see happen and actually making it happen are two very different things.

In a sense, magical thinking is taking optimism to an extreme. You are so optimistic about yourself and your future that you create a story in which magical fantasy trumps any reality. So when you build future plans with that story in mind, you feel good because you anticipate success. Unfortunately, that success may well never occur. The good feelings you have are built on fantasy, which in the psychotherapy world is called a "someday . . . if only . . . " fantasy, which allows you to avoid looking at what you actually have to do, or take real actions, on a concrete level to make your plans happen.

All of us engage in magical thinking, to some extent. Dreaming is part of human nature. Idealizing ourselves, our situations, and our relationships is very common. It is a natural defense; we all need hope to move forward in our lives. For example, romantic love starts on a fabulous shared illusion of mutual idealization, which is later helpful when the going gets rough. Think about when you are really angry at your partner, but can still feel your admiration, attraction, and deep respect for him or her.

When it comes to affluence, problems occur when people start to swap fantasy for reality. They might think, Someday my husband will make more money, or I have had three failed businesses, but someday I will succeed. They are not looking at the facts or having to confront who they really are or what their reality has been. Nor are they likely to create a realistic plan and put in the hard work necessary to turn their ideal or fantasy into reality.

Grasping

Grasping is a Buddhist concept and can be defined as the way in which human beings look toward (or desire) an outside thing or person to fill themselves up, and make them feel content, good about themselves, and complete. Like those who are addicted to consumption, grasping can become an always-hungry animal who is never satisfied for very long. Hank Vyner, M.D., is a physician who left the world of teaching and medical practice to spend more than twenty years living in the Himalayas and conducting interviews with Tibetan lamas on the nature of "Healthy Mind." He offers this definition of grasping:

> The purpose of the Buddhist path is to know the true nature of your mind exactly as it is in every single moment. To this end, Buddhism delineates two kinds of mind activity: the *egocentric* mind and the *egoless* mind. The egocentric mind is engaged in the kind of activity that is familiar to most of us, in which we project concepts onto our experience in the

process of knowing it. This is called in Buddhist terms, grasping—so when the egocentric mind "grasps" a phenomenon, it adds a conceptual level of awareness of that phenomenon that ultimately gets in the way of knowing the true nature of your mind. More specifically, the egocentric mind grasps by projecting three different kinds of concepts onto phenomena in the process of knowing them: (1) conceptions of identity; (2) emotions; and (3) mind films that are recurring cycles of habitual thoughts. The egocentric mind projects these constructs onto itself when it takes any of the following actions: judging, repressing, attaching, or following its own thoughts and feelings.

The egoless mind, in contrast, is able to know its own true nature because it does not engage in "grasping." In Buddhist terms, the egoless mind enables you to realize the emptiness of your own mind, and thus realize your true nature.[1]

Psychologically speaking, how and what we grasp is guided by the deep grooves in our brain that have been created by the habitual ways that we do things. Habit is the great guide of human life (so said David Hume, an empirical philosopher of the eighteenth century), but the brain does not care whether habits are good or bad—it is simply driven to maintain familiar patterns of behavior. People without Affluence Intelligence unconsciously but forcefully protect the patterns that they know and are used to, whether they are heroin addicts, overworked lawyers, or frustrated housewives or househusbands.

Denial

Denial is not always a negative defense. Sometimes we temporarily go into denial to protect ourselves from something we cannot handle immediately, such as a diagnosis of cancer. This form of denial helps us to continue to do what needs to be done instead of being overwhelmed by the reality of a situation.

Whether or not you have Affluence Intelligence impacts on the role denial can play in your life. Let's say an affluent person's wife is threatening to divorce him. He might move into a certain amount of denial about what's happening. If he does not have Affluence Intelligence, he might say, This isn't going to happen, shifting into denial and thereby not doing anything to remedy the situation and inadvertently helping the divorce to take place. But if he has Affluence Intelligence he will say, I don't want this to happen. What can I do to work on this? Instead of using denial, allowing awareness of his wife's feelings (assuming he does not get trapped in negative ruminations or feelings such as despair) will result in him taking steps to try to explore what is going on and potentially repair the marriage. Denial can push feelings away that may be important signals you need to see. Accurately reading the signal being sent will allow you the choice to take positive and effective action.

Without Affluence Intelligence, a person may deny a business situation that is reeling out of control to the point that he or she is on the verge of bankruptcy, saying, The stock market will pick up; we will do better tomorrow. In contrast, a person with Affluence Intelligence will acknowledge the situation, but also knows how to face reality and take action.

Avoidance

Avoidance is more conscious than denial. When you are using avoidance as a defense, you are aware that you are not addressing an issue or situation. An example of avoidance would be: I know that I need to go to the dentist, but I don't want to go. And then not make an appointment. Denial would be, My teeth are fine—I don't need a dentist. Despite being due for a cleaning or having a problem with a tooth.

Another example of avoidance would be, I'm angry with my wife, but I'm not going to talk to her about our problems because it's just too draining. Or, in a business situation, you might avoid addressing a work situation because you don't like confrontation and don't want to have to approach your boss. In both situations, there is a need that you are aware of, but the lack of action (avoidance) allows the situation to perpetuate.

Our client Dennis, who won the lottery, avoided his feelings about his wealth. He wanted to avoid other people, too, because of the discomfort that came up over his money. For the first year after winning the lottery, he stayed overseas in order not to have to deal with anyone. He didn't know what to say to people, or how to spend his time. So he handled his discomfort (or, more honestly, did not deal with it) by avoiding any potentially awkward situations.

David, the architect, was avoiding many hard facts: that the career choices he had made in the past were no longer working for him; that he and his wife were spending more than they were making; that his achievements were not successful enough; that "doing the right thing" was no longer the right thing.

All or Nothing Thinking and Feeling

All or nothing thinking and feeling, a defense psychologists call "splitting," is a means of self-protection in which either oneself or the other person is perceived as all good or all bad. Sometimes people who make use of splitting will build a case against another, citing evidence of all the wrongs done and sins they have committed. At its extreme, a once beloved other can become the enemy. A person employing this defense might, for example, drop a friend after years of loyalty because of one betrayal (or perceived betrayal). On the other extreme, a new lover or boss can be deemed the perfect savior, or "the long-lost missing piece" of oneself.

The use of a black and white mode of thinking, particularly when we are under pressure, leads us to see the world as populated by heroes and villains, winners and losers, perpetrators and victims. It is normal for a child's brain to see the world this way; but at some point during our development through adolescence into adulthood, we should grow out of it. We develop the capacity for integration, enabling us to experience the full range of feelings and thoughts that arise in ourselves and in our relationships. With integration people understand that emotional relationships are complex, more shades of grey than black and white. But people who have a strong vulnerability with integration and who regularly use this defense, when disappointed, will see others as villains and blame them for what has gone wrong, and in so doing, relieve themselves of the pain of looking at their own deficiencies and acknowledging their part in what happened.

Those with Affluence Intelligence are usually more willing to see how people—and life itself—are made up of shades of grey, rather than black and white. Ron, our "people" person from Chapter 2, always gave others the benefit of the doubt and another chance even after they had let him down. When under stress, he would momentarily find himself caught in an all-or-nothing view of a person or conflict, but then he would rapidly see that this perspective was not productive. As a person who is a model of Affluence Intelligence, Ron did not trust his view of situations when he saw them in black and white terms. He knew that seeing the grey areas would result in a more flexible view of any given problem and its potential solutions. He also knew that even when he was truly hurt by a friend or colleague, demonizing him or her was a waste of precious psychic energy.

This is not to say that those with Affluence Intelligence never engage in black and white thinking. Anyone under stress, regardless of his or her capacities, has a tendency to make use of psychological defenses that are akin to the "flight or fight" response of the body's autonomic nervous system. If you feel pushed into a corner, and for a moment it feels like you are truly in danger, you may either attack with everything you've got, or run away as fast as you can. As we have often seen with our clients, when men (in particular) have earned lots of money and their wives don't agree to whatever it is they want to spend it on, they may slip into black and white thinking, such as, Why should I be held back from what I want? I made the money, I should spend it however I want! They can get stuck in that bad place where they cannot see the middle ground, the gradations between black and white. However, they have the ability to quickly bring themselves out of thinking in extremes and find a more nuanced approach to the problem.

Projection

Projection is taking something about yourself that you are uncomfortable with and being critical about that behavior in someone else. Think of the people who gun down doctors who provide abortions while saying, Killing is wrong!

Projection is all about finger-pointing. A man might say, for example, If my wife wasn't so addicted to spending, we would have much more in our retirement account. A woman might say, If my husband would just do x, y, and z at work, he could get a raise and we would be more secure. Their criticisms about one another are not really about what the wife is buying or what the husband is doing at work—it is about their sense of scarcity, and their anxiety and fear about the future. It is an attempt to place the blame for unacceptable thoughts and feelings onto someone else. By assigning the responsibility to another person, we relieve ourselves of the feelings of anxiety, inadequacy, or guilt that we would otherwise have to contend with.

Outside forces that are beyond our control can have an impact on our lives, and blaming these forces is not a case of projection. Our nation's socioeconomic forces have an effect on our own economic well-being. If you, or someone you know, lost a job or a home as a consequence of the Great Recession, then you know just how devastating these forces can be. These losses are a result of an external force, not of the individual's use of defenses. Indeed, it is important to not get mired in self-blame when you have lost your job—particularly when it was not because of your work performance but because your company was downsizing or laying off employees. Being in these circumstances and being upset at the economic conditions that put you there is socially induced powerlessness, not projection. When we talk about projection, we are talking about those people who *always* assign the responsibility for their lack of money and/or success to someone else, saying it was because of their [spouse, parent, boss, etc.] that they're not financially successful or happy.

All of us, including those with Affluence Intelligence, occasionally fall prey to using this defense. Our client Dan projects onto his wife that she has all the power and he is trapped in a prison in his own home. Dan is a very powerful man who makes huge decisions at work every day, but in domestic matters he has a tendency to project his sense of control of his life onto his wife. However, as we see in the lives of those who have unlocked Affluence Intelligence, people like Dan will inevitably move toward taking ownership and responsibility for their situations, and not simply project their uncomfortable feelings onto others.

Being Affected by a Personal History

We each have a sense of who we are that is based on the sum of our personal experiences. Psychoanalytic theory suggests that part of who we are and what we seek is what psychoanalysts have called a *refinding* of the past. Sometimes this refinding serves us. For example, if you had a parent with wonderful qualities (a good listener, a loving person, or someone who was interested in your well-being), you may seek out some of their positive qualities in your choice of a mate.[2] On the other hand, the power of habit and well-entrenched brain groove patterns can result in your refinding some of what was not only familiar, but also negative. We see this in adults who repeat ways they were abused as children in their current family relationships—for example, the adult daughter of an alcoholic who gets involved with another alcoholic.

When you have a childhood or adolescence of a certain type, it strongly informs how you feel about yourself as an adult. If your family did not have money when you were a child, getting money in adulthood can cause serious tension, because you are so removed from where you came from. The impulse is often to return to the familiar and known (that is, poverty). Another way a personal history can affect a person (often women) is if they were told as children that they should not be involved with money, or that talking or thinking about money is unseemly. As adults, they may feel great anxiety when confronted with financial issues. This is true of people who are highly competent in many other aspects of their lives. But somehow, when faced with money issues, they zone out. One of the keys to unlocking Affluence Intelligence is becoming aware of and taking charge of the money-related messages and stories we have heard or have modeled throughout our lives. Otherwise, we are subject to refinding the past, or being in reaction to the refinding of our past.

Having a Negative Cultural or Religious Belief about Money

Along with your personal history, your culture and religion also play important roles in the development of your identity, especially when it comes to financial issues. You may not be able to enjoy money because you have been taught that it is somehow sinful to use money for pleasure. You can use it to house yourself and feed yourself, but not to have fun, to be creative, or to learn.

Culture and religion provide many, if not most, of the people on this planet with an organized set of beliefs about money. To some people, money belongs to God only, and needs to be given back in the form of charity. Some cultures have a prescribed way of understanding the role of money in life—providing a useful structure for handling its emotional challenges. Some cultural beliefs can be used by people to keep their Affluence Intelligence thermostat set on low. For example, the belief that "money is the root of all evil" can play into a person's preexisting anxiety or guilt, increasing the likelihood of self-defeating behaviors. (And by the way, the actual biblical quote is "the *love* of money is the root of all evil." As we have said, the truly affluent enjoy the challenge and the chase and the game of achieving success—a love of money is not the sole motivation for what they do.)

The issue is not whether what you believe is right or wrong. All cultures and religions have their own beauty and wisdom. Rather, the issue is how you, unwittingly, use the beliefs you have been taught that get in the way of turning up the temperature on your Affluence Intelligence thermostat. For example, cultural or religious beliefs can be so powerful that when we do things that seem to violate those beliefs, we may punish ourselves by feeling guilty and depressed, or behave in ways that are ultimately self-destructive.

Those with Affluence Intelligence learn how to work with, over-come, and see beyond self-limiting beliefs of any kind. They can have respect and regard for their religion or culture without letting that respect get in the way of unlocking their Affluence Intelligence and of having a life that is both financially and personally satisfying.

Having a Bias Against the Rich

If you have negative feelings toward the rich (either consciously or unconsciously), you will most likely find unconscious ways to sab-otage your own efforts to accrue wealth. Unfortunately, such be-liefs are all too common.

In her doctoral dissertation, Dr. Joanie Bronfman offers an ex-planation about why it is common to think negatively of those who are wealthy: "The rich are conceptualized as objects devoid of hu-manity, individuality or vulnerability." She goes on to say, "The ob-jectification of the rich assists people to accept their own feelings of envy and hatred and to avoid learning that their myths and pre-conceptions about wealth are not true. For example, they don't dis-cover that some rich people may be motivated by pain and fear. Instead, the assumption is that they are motivated by snootiness and greed." If you have these kinds of negative feelings and beliefs about having wealth, then you may unconsciously undermine or impede resetting your Affluence Intelligence thermostat.

Chances are that you have recognized that you engage in the behaviors of those who have Affluence Intelligence, those who do not, or both. If this is the case, give yourself a pat on the back, be-cause self-awareness is the first step. Right now, your job is to notice without judgment (and perhaps even with a little bemusement) how your mind works—in a manner that is similar to how one ob-serves the workings of the mind when learning how to meditate or focusing on improving your golf game.

Don't rush to judgment if you find you are using defenses that get in your way of learning. Let's say, for example, that you don't like to take risks. There might be several reasons for this. Perhaps the idea of taking risks scares you. Or perhaps it's just not in your personality; it's not your strong suit. This is not necessarily something you have to fix. Remember that defenses of some kind are necessary for you to maintain your psychological equilibrium; they protect you from what you can't handle, and stop you from doing things that may throw the baby out with the bathwater.

In thinking about how and when you use any particular psychological defense, it is important to first determine your baseline—the ways in which you cope with stress and change on a daily basis, both at work and in your personal life. It is true that you may occasionally slip into using a particular defense when your back is against the wall, or when you're in the middle of a battle with a spouse or a child. Almost everyone does. But once you've calmed down, or feel the threat is not as great as you had first thought, then do you continue to use one of the more negative defenses, or do you make use of defenses that are less extreme?

Simply put, your defenses have both a payoff and a price. Once you understand this, you can weigh the payoff against the price and make a conscious decision about whether or not a particular defense serves you. The whole point is about being *conscious* of what you're doing and why you're doing it. Your objective is to manage your defenses so that you maximize your unique personal resources and minimize your obstacles to change. Now, we will give you the tools to make changes in the behaviors that may be holding you back from achieving the affluence that you want and deserve.

chapter nine

DETERMINE YOUR TOTAL AFFLUENCE INTELLIGENCE QUOTIENT

We have been impressed by the high value that our truly affluent clients place on having and following a plan. They are very focused. They use their plan to take action about what comes their way and what happens to them. They are in control of their environment as much as possible (although they also understand that they are never fully in control).

We have been equally struck by how those who have not unlocked their Affluence Intelligence lack a solid, strategic plan. They are far more reactive than proactive, and sometimes they are completely passive. Granted, passivity can sometimes lead to success. Not making a decision and waiting to see what the universe sends you is a certain kind of plan, and has value for some people. You may know people who seem to love not having a plan. They value spontaneity, being "in the flow of what's happening," or believing that any given situation will work out if it is meant to work out. If this gives you the affluence you want, then good. But if it does not, and you complain about having no money and being dissatisfied, then it is likely you are using not having a plan as a defense, as an extension of magical thinking and avoidance. Sometimes, albeit rarely, magic seems to happen when we let go of control and "send it off to the universe." But not having a plan can easily become a way of avoiding the hard work and complex judgments of *having plans and executing them.*

But most of the affluent we know, while being open to opportunity and whatever the universe may send them, do not rely on that alone, because passively waiting for "something" to change usually results in a very long wait. Instead, they have a concrete plan that is shaped as it evolves and develops over time. Our plan will empower you to unlock your Affluence Intelligence and make use of the same capacities that made our clients both happy and successful. By taking leadership of your own life and working this plan, you will discover your own unique way of living the seven components of Affluence Intelligence. Then, like Howard in Chapter 1, you will have that "special something" that brings a smile to your face, a lightness to your heart, and the recognition of those around you that you have Affluence Intelligence.

Your plan will start by determining your Affluence Intelligence Quotient—the sum of the three parts of the Quiz you have completed in the preceding chapters.

Your total score reflects a synergy of attitudes, behaviors, financial effectiveness, and the ability to live your most important priorities. Let's first consider the meaning of this total score.

YOUR AFFLUENCE INTELLIGENCE QUOTIENT:

Total Score Part A   _____

Total Score Part B   _____

Total Score Part C   _____

Affluence Intelligence Quotient (AIQ)   _____

EVALUATING YOUR AIQ SCORES

140 or above	You have 100% of Affluence Intelligence!
120–139	You have very strong resources and alignment of priorities.
110–119	You have strong resources and alignment of priorities.
90–109	You have an average range of resources and alignment of priorities.
80–89	You have a slightly vulnerable range of resources and alignment of priorities.
70–79	You have a very vulnerable range of resources and alignment of priorities.

Profile: High End of the Scoring Continuum (120 or above)

Congratulations! You are in the top AIQ scoring group. You have unlocked Affluence Intelligence and your daily activities reflect your priorities and bring you satisfaction. You fare well in the majority of affluence factors, such as having enough money for your needs and wants; relationships that bring you joy; work you like; being secure; having power, meaning, and purpose; and enjoying the best health you can. Having a high setting on your Affluence Intelligence thermostat means that (for the most part) you have a positive attitude, flexibility in how you handle change, and a sense of overall satisfaction in your life. Your psychological defenses help rather than hinder you from getting what you want. While you may have vulnerabilities in some of your behaviors, attitudes, or in financial effectiveness, your strengths in other areas help to buffer or counterbalance their impact. Your score indicates that you should feel an overall sense of satisfaction in your life, a feeling of affluence. But if you don't feel as affluent as your score seems to indicate, you may wish to look at your areas of strength and focus on those areas that serve you well in your life. You can also go back to the behaviors and attitudes that you did not score as well on and make changes to improve your score. Additionally, you may discover what is getting in your way in Chapter 8.

Profile: Middle of the Scoring Continuum (90–119)

You have scored in the middle range of the Affluence Intelligence Quotient spectrum. The good news is that you have some distinct strengths, and knowing what they are gives you the opportunity to use them with ease. Don't underestimate them or take them for granted; these attitudes and behaviors come easily to you, but it is important to recognize that you are the owner of these strengths and that you can use them to support yourself in challenging times and in times of opportunity. As they say . . . go with your strengths! This means accepting all that is good about who you are, and deciding whether or not you want to raise your Affluence Intelligence thermostat. It may be that your priorities are not where you want them to be. Think about the real versus the ideal. Then take a long, hard look at your vulnerabilities, which are likely to get in the way of your progress. For the specific attitudes and behavior areas with lower scores, you can choose to work on these areas to increase your score, and thereby raise your Affluence Intelligence.

The more areas of strength you have, the more resources you have to handle life situations most effectively. You may choose to be happy with things as they are, or you may choose to work on changing your attitudes and behaviors, in which case you will further unlock your Affluence Intelligence, leading to more life choices and a greater opportunity for attaining financial satisfaction.

Profile: Low End of the Scoring Continuum (Below 90)

Although you may be doing many things in your daily life that reflect your priorities, clearly there is a lot more that you wish you were doing. Your score shows that there is a gap between where you are in your life and where you would like to be, or that some of your attitudes and behaviors may be getting in the way of your own best interests. One or both of these areas would need to change for you to better unlock your Affluence Intelligence. Look at your scores. There may be one or two attitudes and behaviors that need serious thought and consideration. Is it financial ease, resilience, or ambition? Think of these as unused muscles that you need to exercise. Ask yourself if you are being realistic about how much you can take on in a three-month or one-year period. Review Chapter 8, and think about how your defenses are in service of your needs, or how they get in the way of what you say you want for yourself. As you identify defenses or behavioral habits that may be getting in your way, consider new action steps you can take to change. Remember that a low score has nothing to do with intelligence, but it does signal that there is a chance to significantly improve your life.

Perhaps you are willing to accept how your life is now focusing on what you do well, resisting the pressure to have or do more. Your goal can be acceptance and gratitude for what you have. First, think about the internal or external pressures you are under to do things differently. It may be that you have an idealized view of how you think things should be in your life. Or, in the interest of being scrupulously honest, perhaps you were too critical of yourself during the Affluence Intelligence Quotient test. Review your answers and see if you might have been giving yourself a hard time.

Keep in mind:

- If your Affluence Intelligence Quotient is in the very high or very low range, we recommend that you have a close friend, partner, or spouse take the quiz on your behalf. It may be that you are being overly grand or positive, or overly humble or negative in appraising your own attitudes and behaviors. You can compare your scores to that of your friend's scores and average them to get a more realistic score.
- Defenses: Now that you know your strengths and vulnerabilities, you will benefit from reading Chapter 8 on defenses. Ask yourself:
  - › How do my defenses help support how I see myself as a person, my unique personality? How do my defenses help me cope with stress and change? Which of my defenses are allies in my daily life?
  - › How do my particular defenses get in my way of attaining Affluence Intelligence, keeping me stuck in the same old thought patterns and behaviors?

Understand that the defenses that once worked for you may no longer fit who you are and what you want in your life today, as well as what you desire for your future.

Let's look at a couple of client stories, seeing how the clients' individual strengths and vulnerabilities are revealed in their AI quotients.

Katie
Part A: Lifestyle Priorities Gap score of 6 = 30 points
Part B: Behaviors and Attitudes = 57 points
Part C: Financial Effectiveness = 9 points
Affluence Intelligence Quotient = 96 points (midrange)

CHART 9.1 PART A: KATIE'S LIFESTYLE PRIORITIES
AND GAP SCORE

	Step 1: Today	Step 2: One year from today	Step 3: Difference
PROSPERITY	6	5	1
PEOPLE	2	3	1
PRODUCTIVITY/WORK	1	1	0
PRODUCTIVITY/OTHER	3	2	1
PASSION	4	6	2
PEACE	5	4	1

Step 4: Total Difference

GAP Number = 6

(30 points)

CHART 9.2 PART B: KATIE'S BEHAVIORS AND
ATTITUDES

	Scores
1. Resilience	6
2. Assertiveness	9
3. Interpersonal effectiveness	9
4. Ability to work hard	6
5. Optimism	6
6. Open mindedness	9
7. Sense of control of one's life	8
8. Ambition	4
TOTAL PART B SCORE:	5
	7

CHART 9.3 PART C: KATIE'S FINANCIAL
EFFECTIVENESS

	Scores
1. Financial Competency	4.5
2. Financial Ease	4.5
TOTAL PART C SCORE:	9

Katie is a forty-eight-year-old single mother who works as an administrator in social services. She is a vibrant woman with an active social life who is psychologically savvy and easygoing. Her many friends see her as someone they can trust and rely upon. (This is reflected in one of her top priorities: people.) She spends a lot of time maintaining her relationships.

Her income is just enough to cover her expenses. She, like many, took a hit in the Great Recession, losing significant equity in her home. She is saving for her daughter's college education, and those savings have been depleted by the recession. She worries that she may not have enough money for her daughter's college years.

Since Katie was in her early teens, she knew she wanted to be in a service profession helping people who are in trouble or in need. She was trained as a counselor, and has worked in that field for twenty years. Katie feels that, given the limitations of employment in the public sector, she has a relatively good job. She likes the people, but has little opportunity for career advancement or expansion of her skills. Consequentially, she has started to get a little bored. In order to make more money, she has started an animal training business, reflecting her passion for animals.

Katie has a dream of retiring to the country. She'd like to buy some land and build a simple home in a community of friends. As she is nearing her fiftieth birthday, she has become aware that she is not reaching her goals. Five years ago she left a fifteen-year marriage and has not found a new life partner. She would like to feel more peace. She wants to take better care of her health. She has chronic back problems and would like to take up yoga and get massage treatments more frequently. She has a great relationship with her daughter, who is a high school senior, but Katie is now facing an empty nest.

Katie has never been a good money manager and always complains that she doesn't make enough, but money has never been a big priority for her. She has trouble thinking through the long-term impact of her larger investments. Katie scored high on open-mindedness and interpersonal effectiveness, which fits well with her choice of career in the counseling/human relations field. It was more puzzling that her assertiveness was high given the fact that she didn't ask for a raise when she took over her boss's job. Here we can see that her assertiveness may be influenced by her low scores on financial effectiveness and her ranking of prosperity, which may have influenced her to accept management's statement—without question—that there was no room in the budget for a raise. Or perhaps this reflects her low scores on ambition, which may have gotten in her way of asking for a raise.

Clearly, Katie needs to improve on financial effectiveness if she wants to reach prosperity. Like many of us, Katie made a career choice that reflects her existing strengths, but it is not a career that has moved her forward on increasing prosperity. This is not uncommon among those who find a niche in the world of work that is comfortable and provides sustenance, but does not stretch them in ways that would increase their bottom line.

While she has as strong command of herself, her scores on resilience and working hard may be worth her attention, given these capacities may have an impact on her reaching her desired changes in priorities. Katie realizes that she may not achieve her dreams if she doesn't have more money, but she has always made decisions based on meaning and purpose, not money. Katie is now at a crossroads in how she uses her time and expends her life energy—will she be willing to change her lifestyle priorities, commit time and energy to becoming more prosperous, which means less time for other pursuits—such as moving people and passion to a lower priority?

David

Part A: Lifestyle Priorities Gap score of 12 = 20 points
Part B: Behaviors and Attitudes = 62 points
Part C: Financial Effectiveness = 16 points
Affluence Intelligence Quotient = 98 points (midrange)

Unlike Katie, who was limited in how much she could earn because of the nature of her job, David (the architect we met in Chapter 1) had much more potential for financial growth. David's Affluence Intelligence quotient showed how specific attitudes and behaviors had gotten in the way of him unlocking his Affluence Factor. Although he was ambitious and a hard worker, he no longer felt in charge of his life. His difficulties with interpersonal issues had taken a toll. He had been reluctant to assert himself at work, and had not been skillful about handling his feelings, particularly when he was in conflict with another person. His scores on optimism and assertiveness showed vulnerability that would make it hard for him to be more hopeful and to take risks. While David understood accounting, he was not particularly at ease with money. As we described in Chapter 1, he felt inadequate, if not defeated, about having enough to keep up the lifestyle of those in his community and to provide the things he believed his wife wanted and needed. David wanted to reset his Affluence Intelligence thermostat to increase the priorities of peace, prosperity, and passion.

His Affluence Intelligence quotient showed a perfect storm with one area of behavioral or attitudinal vulnerability colluding with another, leading to his sense of failure and anxiety. His lack of a

CHART 9.4 PART A: DAVID'S LIFESTYLE PRIORITIES
AND GAP SCORE

	Step 1: Today	Step 2: One year from today	Step 3: Difference
PROSPERITY	5	2	3
PEOPLE	3	6	3
PRODUCTIVITY/WORK	1	1	0
PRODUCTIVITY/OTHER	2	5	3
PASSION	4	3	1
PEACE	6	4	2
		Step 4: Total Difference	GAP Number = 12 (20 points)

CHART 9.5 PART B: DAVID'S BEHAVIORS AND
ATTITUDES

	Scores
1. Resilience	9
2. Assertiveness	6
3. Interpersonal effectiveness	7
4. Ability to work hard	9
5. Optimism	7
6. Open mindedness	8
7. Sense of control of one's life	7
8. Ambition	9
TOTAL PART B SCORE:	6
	2

CHART 9.6 PART C: DAVID'S FINANCIAL
EFFECTIVENESS

	Scores
1. Financial Competency	9
2. Financial Ease	7
TOTAL PART C SCORE:	**16**

personal sense of control in his life made him feel that he was only a cog in the machine of his life—the life he was leading did not reflect who he was or wanted to be.

David looked at the results of his test and was stunned—not by the profile of his strengths and weaknesses, but by the realization that what he was doing in both his marriage and at work was self-defeating. He saw that he had lost control of his choices and of the direction of his life. His anxiety and negative attitude were causing him to lose hope and to lose sleep. David recognized that he needed to make changes, or risk continuing the downward spiral of his current Affluence Intelligence profile.

So David decided that it was time to increase his Affluence Intelligence. In his words, "It just isn't worth it. I'm running so hard in circles, my knees are buckling, and I'm not going anywhere that I want to go. I want to at least try to live my strengths and do what I enjoy."

Katie and David were excited when we explained that, unlike your regular IQ, which is pretty much fixed, your Affluence Intelligence quotient can be changed. And chances are you'd like to raise yours, too. Read on.

chapter ten

CREATE YOUR OWN AFFLUENCE PLAN AND TURN UP YOUR THERMOSTAT

*N*ow that you know your AI quotient and are aware of the defenses and beliefs that might be getting in your way, it's time to create an action plan to unlock your Affluence Intelligence. We will take you through the Affluence Intelligence three-month plan—a step-by-step program that will show you exactly how to turn up your thermostat. This plan makes use of the lessons we have learned from our very successful affluent clients.

SETTING THE STAGE: BEFORE YOU TAKE ACTION

Having the right mindset is crucial to success. Your intentions need to be aligned with your actions, so that the steps you take toward your goal are taken with clarity and purpose. Let's start by asking you the same thing we ask of our clients, which is to get into "retreat mode"—to give yourself a break (for at least three hours) from phones, e-mail, and routines, and put any decision making about your money or lifestyle on hold. The purpose is to give yourself the time and space to become fully aware of your thoughts and feelings, not what other people want or expect you to think and feel.

Specifically, we tell clients to:

- Take a step back from your everyday routine, relax, and look at the big picture of your money and your life. Give yourself the freedom to think outside of what you define as normal, to freely consider and review your attitudes, beliefs, and expectations about your money and your life.
- Imagine that it is three months from now. In looking back at the past three months, what would you like to have accomplished in order to not have regrets?
- Imagine it is one year from now. In looking back over the past year, what steps did you have to take in order to not have regrets about where you are?
- Imagine it is ten years from now. In looking back on the last decade, what steps did you have to take in order to not have regrets about where you are?

When you allow yourself to dream (whether it be three months, one year, or ten years from now) without judging or censoring yourself, you may be surprised by what you discover. In giving yourself permission to observe your life free of judgments and expectations (yours and others), you never know what you might find out about yourself.

We have a client who took over the management of the family business, a drugstore in a small midwestern town, when his father passed away. Everyone in the town, and in his family, expected him to be a true "heir" of this business. After a year, he felt bored and stuck. While he had always expected to run the store, and was in fact doing a satisfactory job, he said, "This just isn't me." When he asked his three closest friends what he should do they all said the same thing: "You love the outdoors. You love to build things, and you're very good at it. If your parents didn't have this readymade job for you, what would you want to do?" He got a contractor's license and a real estate license. He went on to become a successful real estate developer, and his new life plan allowed him to "do work he liked so much that he lost track of time" and to "have enough money for his needs and wants"—two of the seven elements of Affluence Intelligence.

Find an Affluence Intelligence buddy. Our client's friends were instrumental to his awakening from feeling bored and stuck to finding his true career path. You don't have to do your plan all on your own. We recommend that you choose a trustworthy friend, partner, or colleague to keep your plan on track. The agreement with your AI buddy should include a minimum, once-weekly review of your progress, as well as the obstacles you have encountered as you have implemented your AI plan. Most importantly, empower your AI buddy to be empathic and keep you honest— while he or she needs to have an empathic ear, they will not let you make excuses for why you haven't followed through on your plan.

CREATING YOUR THREE-MONTH AFFLUENCE INTELLIGENCE PLAN

The following steps will build on your Affluence Intelligence quotient, draw on your awareness of what may be holding you back from affluence, and help you to turn up your Affluence Intelligence thermostat to achieve the life you are meant to live.

Step One: List the Areas of your AI Quotient You Want to Change

- Priorities
- Attitudes
- Behaviors
- Financial effectiveness

Start with the results of your Affluence Intelligence quotient test from Chapter 9. Look at your lifestyles priorities chart and make a list of the priorities you want to shift in the next three months, to begin to close the gap, moving you toward your desired priorities. You can list this on a separate piece of paper, or create a document in your computer's word-processing program. Next, look at your scores on the attitudes and behavior part of the Affluence Intelligence quotient quiz and choose the attitudes and behaviors that you want to strengthen. Then look at your scores on financial competency and financial ease and choose the capacities you want to improve for financial effectiveness.[1] Making changes in your life is like planning a road trip. You would not get in your car and drive around aimlessly, hoping that by sheer luck you would get where you wanted to go. Instead, you would get out a map and pinpoint your ultimate destination, make a plan as to how you will get there, and only then get in your car and go.

When Katie, the single working mother, reviewed how she had rated her priorities, she saw that she wanted to increase passion, productivity (other), and prosperity. On the attitudes and behaviors part of the quiz, she saw that she wanted to increase her scoring on the areas of financial effectiveness, ambition, and optimism.

Step Two: Make a Values Statement

In this step, you will create values statements for the priorities, attitudes, and behaviors you have listed in Step One. These values statements will be the guiding principles for raising your Affluence Intelligence thermostat, an expression of your personal mission for the next three months, and where you want to be at the end of one year.

As you consider your priorities, attitudes, and behaviors, and capacity for financial effectiveness, answer the following questions:

- Why is this priority, attitude, behavior, or attaining financial effectiveness important to you?
- What is the highest purpose of it for you?
- What will it help bring into your life?

Once you have answered these questions after careful thought, write out a statement that might follows this format:

1. I value _____ (priority, attitude, behavior, or financial effectiveness) because it _____.

2. Achieving this priority, or increasing/developing this attitude, behavior, or financial effectiveness of _____ will move me toward having _____(name one of the seven elements of affluence here).

> ### The 7 Elements of Affluence
> 1. Having enough money to meet both your needs and your desires.
> 2. Doing work you like so much you lose track of time.
> 3. Having relationships that bring you joy.
> 4. Being safe in body and mind.
> 5. Having power.
> 6. Living a life that has meaning and purpose.
> 7. Enjoying and maintaining good health.

For example, you might say, "I value *peace* because it *brings me a sense of balance in my life.* Achieving *peace* would move me toward enjoying and maintaining better physical and emotional health."

Katie's value statements for the behaviors and attitudes she targeted were as follows.

Financial competency

"I value *financial competency* because I want to attain financial security. Achieving financial competency will move me toward *having enough money for my needs and wants.*"

Financial ease

"I value *financial ease* so that I am more comfortable with money. Achieving financial ease will move me toward *having enough money for my needs and wants.*"

Optimism

"I value *optimism* because I want to have more positive experiences with people in my life. Achieving greater optimism will move me toward *relationships that bring me joy.*"

Ambition

"I value *ambition* because it will help me to develop a successful business. Increasing ambition will move me toward *having enough money for my needs and wants.*"

Productivity (work)

"I value *productivity* in order to live my passion in my animal training business. Achieving productivity will move me toward *doing work I like so much that I lose track of time.*"

Prosperity

"I value *prosperity* because it will help me to live my dream of living in the country. Achieving prosperity will move me toward *a life of meaning and purpose.*"

Productivity (other)

"I value *productivity* with the goal of increasing self-care in my daily life in order to *enjoy the best health I can.*"

Step Three: Set Goals

Set a specific goal for each of your value statements, such as, "For the next three months, I will exercise every other day." In setting your goals, you need to strike a balance between setting the most optimistic goals possible, and setting a goal that is too easy, leaving you exactly where you are right now. If you try to change too much, you may be setting yourself up for failure; too little and you won't see enough change. Your goal could be anything that helps you make a significant step toward a career change, a lifestyle change, or a financial change, such as an increase in your personal assets.

The most challenging aspect of setting goals is having the opportunity to think outside your usual box. To kick-start your process, keep the following in mind:

1. Ask yourself, If I were doing what I really wanted to do, what would I be doing that is different from my regular activities? What do I want more of, or less of, in my daily life?

2. Beware of stopping yourself before you start. Don't discount your idea by saying, "My goal is not possible." You can decide whether or not that is true later. Right now you are exploring possibilities that you ordinarily would not consider.

3. Don't worry about solving problems immediately, or arriving at solutions quickly. Many of us have a tendency to move from talking about an issue or problem into instantly trying to find a solution. In the race to fix a problem, we often do not fully understand what the problem is really about, or, at a deep level, what we really want. Simply put, most of us are under so much pressure to "get on and do it" that we short-circuit the discovery process, resulting in our knowing only part of what we think, feel, need, or want. As facilitators of this strategy for more than a decade, we know all too well that unless participants have really allowed themselves the freedom to speak their minds, the process will ultimately be limited in scope and impact. You can also ask your Affluence Intelligence buddy to review your goals to see that you are reaching for what is most important to you.

Chart 10.1 shows the goals that Katie set.

CHART 10.1   KATIE'S VALUES AND GOALS

Katie's AI Areas of Desired Change	Value Statements	Set Goals	Action Steps	Defenses that Get in My Way
Financial competency	I value *financial competency* because I want to attain financial security. Achieving financial competency will move me toward *having enough money for my needs and wants.*	Learn the financial basics about having and managing a financial plan. Increase my knowledge about investment opportunities.		
Optimism	I value *optimism* because I want to have more positive experiences with people in my life. Achieving greater optimism will move me toward relationships that bring me joy.	Exercise greater optimism in my relationships with my partner and my children.		
Prosperity	I value *prosperity* in order to live my dream of living in the country. Achieving prosperity will move me toward *a life of meaning and purpose.*	Develop a business plan for my animal training enterprise.		
Productivity (other)	I value *productivity* with the goal of increasing self-care in my daily life in order to *enjoy good health.*	Practice new self-care activities that I will begin next week and will commit to doing for at least 90 days.		

Step Four: Choosing Action Steps

Once you have identified your goals, you will need to develop a series of action steps, specific tasks that will move you toward a successful outcome. The Affluence Intelligence three-month plan requires you to complete between one and three action steps in each of the key areas you selected from your AI analysis: priorities, attitudes, behaviors, and financial effectiveness. These action steps continue every month for three months, starting with the upcoming week. For example, if you want more peace in your life, decide on the three action steps you can take (for example, taking a walk twice a week, going to church, or saying no to seeing friends who deplete you emotionally) that will begin to unlock your Affluence Intelligence and move you toward your goal.

When it comes to choosing the steps in your action plan, we recommend that you start small. We have learned that being conservative in goal setting will more likely lead to success. Small steps will provide a foundation for change. For example, if you want to exercise more than your usual once a week workout, we suggest that you create a modest goal of exercising three times a week rather than aiming for working out five to seven times per week. We want you to experience the payoff of success, one that you can build on, rather than missing the mark and having another "What's the point of even trying?" experience that may cause you to give up.

The reason that small successes can have such a powerful effect is that doing something concrete toward your goal is important. You have demonstrated to yourself that you are capable of this behavior. Once you start moving forward, you may find that the changes you have decided to make are not only possible, but also enjoyable. You may also be surprised by the positive feedback and support you get from people in your life. For example, we work with a couple where the woman is very assertive, but the man (the wealth holder) is not. James is passive aggressive, holding his anger underneath a mask of pleasantness. He was scared to assert himself with his wife, Karen, because he feared her reaction (that she would use it against him). Actually, the truth was that James was telling himself a false story based on the experiences he had had in his family of origin. When he finally did assert himself, Karen was actually fine with it. He saw that the world hadn't come to an end, and it changed his perspective on whether or not it was safe to be assertive with her.

At times creating change in your life may require making just the right amount of adjustments. Sometimes when you change your behaviors you may go too far in the opposite direction. You want to make sure the pendulum does not swing from all to nothing. It's best to strive for the middle ground.

Remember, other people may not be happy or comfortable about the changes you make. If, for example, you have let someone take advantage of you and then you begin to become assertive, they may not like your new attitude because they may have to start compromising or not get their way all of the time. That's okay. The changes that you are making are because of an important agreement that you have made with yourself, so at times, you must be willing to put up with others' resistance or discomfort in order to make positive changes in your life.

Before choosing the tactical action steps you will take, please remember that it's your personal mission, driven by your values statements, that is the heart of your action plan. You will unlock Affluence Intelligence when your choices and actions are aligned with your deepest and most important values. Ultimately, raising your Affluence Intelligence thermostat means gaining greater affluence on your terms—living a life that reflects your values and your life dreams. Keep your eye on the highest purpose and goal: unlocking Affluence Intelligence and living a life that maximizes your capacity to live its seven attributes.

As you set up and move forward on your three-month Affluence Intelligence plan, consider the following:

- For three months, break your goals down into small, achievable steps. Start with a first step that you will commit to taking. For example, you want to improve your exercise routine by working out one more time per week. The first step is to pick the hour and day of week you will do it. Put this on your calendar with the same commitment it would have if it were a medical appointment. Set a timeline for your action steps on your three-month action plan, and post it on your refrigerator or bulletin board in plain sight.
- Visualize yourself achieving your goals, as well as successfully taking the action steps in your current life.
- Set regular times (at least once weekly) to check your progress—meaning that you confirm that you have done what you have said you were going to do—in whatever calendar method you use (such as a PDA, Day-Timer, and so on).

To help you create your three-month Affluence Intelligence plan, in the next chapter you will find a planning chart with practical suggestions for concrete steps that you can take toward changing the areas of your Affluence Intelligence that you want to work on. Feel free to use these as they are, or as a guideline for creating action steps that will better suit your lifestyle and goals.

Katie decided on the following steps for her three-month Affluence Intelligence plan:

1. Financial Effectiveness

- Meet with my financial advisor to plan for the next year.
- Take a one-day course on Finance 101 through my local junior college.
- Say no to myself and others when it comes to spending money for the next three months on wants not basic needs.

2. Productivity (other)

- Commit to doing a yoga class at my YMCA three times a week.
- Cut back on dinners with friends to save time as well as money.
- Take at least fifteen minutes every day to take a walk, window shop, or read a novel.

3. Prosperity

- In the next thirty days, meet with a good friend who is a business coach who can help me develop a plan for my animal training business. Develop a plan that grows the business at a pace that does not impede my current job performance or damage my health.
- Set realistic goals regarding the number of clients I will have and the amount of money I need and want to make every month.

4. Optimism

- Every Monday morning for the next three months, spend ten minutes focusing on how, if I keep a positive attitude, things can turn out well.
- Start a journal of optimism and list ways I can be more optimistic, and the outcome of my efforts.

- When I start to feel cynical or find myself engaging in negative self-talk, stop the internal dialogue and shift from an attitude of scarcity to one of possibility.
- Give myself credit for noticing when I engage in negative talk.
- Find a friend who will be willing to be my Affluence Intelligence buddy, to talk with weekly and who will monitor my progress.

Step Five: Identify the Defenses that Get In Your Way

In this step you will identify how you have gotten in your own way in the past. Below is a list of the psychological defenses we discussed in Chapter 8. Think about which of these you typically use in regard to making changes in your life. For example, you may typically say to yourself, "I don't have the time" (denial; telling yourself a false story), or "I don't make enough money, so I don't deserve more peace" (all or nothing thinking).

To review, here are common defenses. Check those that you suspect may apply to you:

- ❑ Telling yourself a false story
- ❑ Keeping up appearances
- ❑ Magical thinking
- ❑ Grasping
- ❑ Denial
- ❑ Avoidance
- ❑ All or nothing thinking and feeling
- ❑ Projection
- ❑ Not having a strategic plan
- ❑ Being affected by personal history
- ❑ Having a negative culture or religious belief about money
- ❑ Having a bias against the rich

If you want to raise your thermostat and unlock your Affluence Intelligence, it is crucial for you to know and own responsibility for the impact your defenses can have on your ability to change. We have been impressed by many of our wealthy clients who admit their mistakes and acknowledge how their defenses have gotten in their way. Taking responsibility for your defenses does not mean you have to go through a personality makeover—it simply means that by knowing your vulnerabilities, you can take charge of their impact on your life.

In order to "get out of your own way," you can try these four simple steps:

1. **Notice** that you are responding in your usual, defensive style.
2. **Stop** the action (stop old patterns).
3. **Pause** and step back and make a choice to change.
4. **Change** your behavior and follow your new action plan.

Human beings may be stubborn about maintaining patterns, but with persistence and determination (remember, you can "walk through walls"), and by taking small incremental steps, you will raise your Affluence Intelligence thermostat and start new, more affluent life patterns (see Chart 10.2 for the next portion of Katie's plan).

Filling in Your Chart

Now complete the following chart on how you will raise your Affluence Intelligence thermostat for the next three months. (Remember, you don't have to fill in the whole chart, just choose the particular priorities, attitudes, behaviors, financial effectiveness you want to change.)

CHART 10.2—KATIE'S ACTION STEPS AND DEFENSES

Katie's AI Areas of Desired Change	Value Statements	Goals	Action Steps	Defenses that Get in My Way
Financial competency	I value *financial competency* because I want to attain financial security. Achieving financial competency will move me toward *having enough money for my needs and wants.*	Learn the financial basics about having and managing a financial plan. Increase my knowledge about investment opportunities.	Meet with my financial advisor to plan for the next year. Take a one-day course on Finance 101 through my local community college. Say no to myself and others when it comes to spending money for the next 6 months.	Avoidance by procrastination. Telling myself the false story that all the activities that keep me busy get in the way of achieving this goal.
Optimism	I value *optimism* because I want to have more positive experiences with people in my life. Achieving greater optimism will move me toward relationships that bring me joy.	Exercise greater optimism in my relationships with my partner and my children.	Every Monday morning for the next three months, I will spend 10 minutes focusing on how, if I keep a positive attitude, things can turn out well. Start a journal of optimism and list ways I can be more optimistic, and the outcome of my efforts. When I start to feel cynical or find myself engaging in negative self-talk, stop the internal dialogue and shift from an attitude of scarcity to one of possibility. Give myself credit for noticing when I engage in negative talk.	Telling myself the false story that "it is too late in my life to be more optimistic," or refinding my past attitude of "I can't do it, and it won't work."
Prosperity	I value *prosperity* in order to live my dream of living in the country. Achieving prosperity will move me toward *a life of meaning and purpose.*	Develop a business plan for my animal training enterprise.	In the next 30 days, meet with a good friend who is a business coach who can help me develop a plan for my animal training business. Develop a plan that grows the business at a pace that is does not impede my current job performance or that is damaging to my health. Set realistic goals regarding the amount: of clients I need and want to make every month.	Avoidance. Not having a strategic plan. Magical thinking: it will succeed if the universe intends it to. Setting goals that are unrealistic in which I end up feeling like it was all a waste of time and I'm a failure at business.
Productivity (other)	I value *productivity* with the goal of increasing self-care in my daily life in order to *enjoy good health.*	Practice new self-care activities that I will begin next week and will commit to doing for at least 90 days	Commit to doing a yoga class at my local YMCA three times a week. Cut back on dinners with friends to save time as well as money. Take at least 15 minutes every day to take a walk, window shop, or read a novel.	Avoidance by means of procrastination. Not having a strategic plan.

THE AFFLUENCE INTELLIGENCE
JOURNEY OF LEARNING

Raising your Affluence Intelligence thermostat is a journey. And this journey requires learning new habits and ways of thinking. Our clients have taught us the importance of maximizing the use of personal strengths and virtues. Generally speaking, our clients do not fight who they are. Instead, they fully use who they are to get what they want and to learn in the ways that best work for them. Through identifying your learning styles and your learning pace, you will be able to capitalize on your strengths and improve your self-advocacy skills. This will help you forward in your journey. In contrast, if you try to learn in ways that do not come naturally to you, it will be like trying to force a round peg into a square hole, and you will set yourself up for failure.

Your Learning Style

As you may have realized from your own educational experiences, people have different styles of learning new material and information. Most people will have a strong preference about how they best learn. Take a look at the learning styles outlined below and see which most suits you. As you continue on your journey toward affluence, seek out information in the manner that you will best be able to learn it. For example, if you are an auditory learner and want to learn more about an issue, seek out material in CD format.

The Visual Learning Style

People with a visual learning style use visual images such as pictures, charts, maps, and graphs to learn. They find it easiest to grasp challenging concepts by making visual representations of those ideas. If you are a visual learner, you may find yourself making pictures or doodles to make note of your thoughts during a meeting

CHART 10.3—YOUR THREE-MONTH AFFLUENCE INTELLIGENCE PLAN

	Value Statement(s)	Goals	Action Steps	Defenses that get in my way
Peace	Peace is an important value because_____.			
Passion	Passion is an important value because_____.			
Productivity (work)	Productivity (work) is an important value because_____.			
Productivity (other)	Productivity (other) is an important value because_____.			
People	People is an important value because_____.			
Prosperity	Prosperity is an important value because_____.			
Resilience				

Priorities

Behaviors	**Assertiveness**			
	Ability to work hard and achieve goals			
	Interpersonal effectiveness			
Attitudes	**Optimism**			
	Open mindedness and curiosity			
	Ability to take control over one's life			
	Ambition			
Financial Effectiveness	**Financial competency**			
	Financial ease			

or brainstorming session. You may also use graphs, films, video games, or photographs to help you understand things.

The Auditory Learning Style

People with an auditory learning style prefer to hear rather than see in order to process information. Generally speaking, they love to speak and they love to listen. They are good at making speeches and presentations, and enjoy going to lectures. They often create musical jingles or mnemonics to help them memorize things and prefer to speak about things rather than write about them. If you are an auditory learner, you may use storytelling or jokes to make a point.

The Verbal Learning Style

People with a verbal learning style find it easiest to express themselves in both the written and the spoken word. They love reading, writing, and word games such as tongue twisters, rhymes, limericks, and so on. They learn best through books, magazines, reading online, and newspapers. If you are a verbal learner, you know the meaning of many words, are always learning new words, and are eager to use these words in conversation with others.

The Physical Learning Style

People with a physical learning style like to use their bodies and their sense of touch to learn. They often like sports and exercise, and other physical activities such as gardening or woodworking. They can think things out best when active. They would rather fix a car by tinkering around with the engine than by reading the owner's manual.

The Logical Learning Style

People with a logical learning style enjoy logical and mathematical reasoning. It's easy for them to find connections between seemingly unrelated ideas or to understand seemingly meaningless patterns. They are good at math and can often solve advanced mathematical problems in their heads. It is important for them to understand the rational sequence of what they are learning. If you are a logical learner, you may use these skills to set budgets and create to-do lists, which you typically number and rank before taking action on them.

The Social Learning Style

People with a social learning style can communicate well with other people. They may enjoy mentoring or counseling others. They typically prefer learning in groups or in classes, surrounded by others.

If you are a social learner, you prefer social activities over doing your own thing. You probably like to stay after class and talk to other students, and you enjoy games that involve other people such as card games, basketball, or baseball.

The Solitary Learning Style

People with a solitary learning style are private, introspective, and independent. They are aware of their own thinking, and may analyze the different ways they think and feel. They spend time on self-analysis, and often reflect on past events and the way they handled them. They may keep a journal or diary to record their thoughts.

If you are a solitary learner, you may have read self-help books or listened to tapes made by seminar or workshop leaders. You prefer to work on problems by retreating to somewhere quiet and working through possible solutions (so much so, in fact, that you may want to keep in mind that there are times when the solution might be more easily solved by talking to someone else).

Your Pace of Learning

Some people get overwhelmed if they try too many new things at once, and therefore need to learn slowly. Others like to learn at a faster pace in order to maintain a sense of excitement and to keep from getting bored. Think back to past learning experiences such as college, an adult education evening class, or when a friend was trying to teach you a new skill, like motorcycle repair or bread baking. Did you approach it carefully, or did you dive right in? Did you try to learn everything you could about the subject at once, or did you learn methodically, wanting to fully understand one concept before moving on to the next? Did you immerse yourself, or did you find yourself needing frequent breaks? Think of some concrete examples to understand what has worked best for you in the past.

It is vital that you make sure your action steps are aligned with both your learning styles and your pace of learning. Of course, there is no one right way to learn and these learning styles are often used in combination. For example, you might be both a logical and solitary learner who can learn quickly. Or you might be an auditory and social learner who likes to learn slowly.

Through identifying both your learning style and the best pace for your learning, you will understand which of these styles work best for you. By using the most effective styles and techniques, you will be able to maximize your success with the Affluence Intelligence plan, turning up your Affluence Intelligence thermostat.

Executive Functioning and Attention Deficit

Some people have cognitive issues that affect their capacity to learn and to complete tasks. These learning issues include the well-known diagnosis of Attention Deficit Disorder (ADD) or Attention Deficit Hyperactivity Disorder (ADHD), and other problems with the executive component of brain functioning. If you have, or believe you may have, some of these issues, do not despair. There are psychometric tests that can help pinpoint the nature of the problem, and many modalities of treatment that can resolve the issue, including medications, therapy, and tutoring that can help you to work around the issue that is getting in your way. We strongly recommend that you take charge and seek appropriate professional care. There are many, many people who have Affluence Intelligence who have learned to live with or work around these prewired cognitive issues. The most important step to take is to get an accurate diagnosis, and then to seek out state-of-the-art help.

Acceptance

After doing this work and introspection you may come to the realization that your life is fine as it is and, at least for the next year, you do not need to change it. Maybe you picked up this book because you feel pressure from outside forces—perhaps a spouse, or society in general—to make more and have more, whereas actually what you really need to do is to recognize and be grateful for what you already have.

If discovering your Affluence Intelligence quotient has allowed you to see that the life you have now is the good life, and that your personal mission is to more fully embrace what is good, and not worry about what is missing, then we suggest that you choose acceptance: to live with and enjoy who you are, accepting your current status without having to resort to grasping or endless rumination about what is wrong in your life or to be controlled by "someday, if only" fantasies.

Acceptance means taking a stand about yourself, and to unlock your Affluence Intelligence by deepening your appreciation of exactly who you are. If you neither take the step of acceptance nor decide to increase your Affluence Intelligence thermostat, you may suffer in an endless cycle of uncertainty and ambivalence, ultimately *lowering* your Affluence Intelligence thermostat.

Acceptance means acknowledging that you have reached a "good enough" place in your life. You have decided that you don't need "more"—people, money, things—and that you can embrace and enjoy who you are and what you have right now. This does not mean that you are giving up. Giving up is very different from acceptance—it does not include self-love, or a deep appreciation of how your life is already a good life.

Acceptance is appropriate for some people and not others. Peggy and Elise both scored low in the attitudes and behavior quiz on interpersonal effectiveness. Peggy's priority was prosperity. She realized that her lack of interpersonal effectiveness might be the reason that she was not getting the promotion she wanted at work that would increase her salary—her boss said that a couple of her coworkers had mentioned she could be "prickly." Because much of her work involved interacting with the public, she decided that her people skills—her interpersonal effectiveness—was something she wanted and needed to change to unlock her Affluence Intelligence. Peggy crafted a value statement to illuminate her personal mission: "I value developing my interpersonal skills to have greater satisfaction in my relationships and to increase my financial affluence." With this value in mind, she created a concrete action plan. Because she had identified that she was someone who liked to learn in a group, she joined a class on people skills at her local adult education center. The class involved role playing, which Peggy enjoyed and found very helpful. By defining her personal mission (the values statement) and then raising her Affluence Intelligence thermostat by learning new people skills, both her coworkers and the company's customers liked Peggy much better, and she eventually got the promotion that she wanted. She also found that her improved skills made for more satisfying friendships.

In contrast, Elise had suspected in the past that her people skills were not very good—she had argued with a neighbor, and was estranged from one of her children. But her priority was peace, not prosperity. Peace for her was being alone with a book, or going for a long swim in the local pool—actions that did not require a lot of people skills. Because her work was graphic design, which was done primarily over the Internet with very little interaction with clients, she decided that she could simply accept, for the foreseeable future, her current level of interpersonal effectiveness. She chose instead to focus her time and energy on other areas that she wanted to improve, such as resilience.

Reaching your full Affluence Intelligence requires a multifaceted journey. You may decide to focus on raising your thermostat in some areas, while accepting where you are in others. Stick with it, and have faith in both yourself and the process. You are opening yourself up to a future of enormous possibility—a future of affluence.

chapter eleven

THE NEXT THREE MONTHS: PUTTING YOUR PLAN INTO PRACTICE

*Y*ou have decided to raise your AIQ and have set goals in each of the four areas of Affluence Intelligence: Priorities, Behaviors, Attitudes, and Financial Effectiveness. Now it is time to create your personal AI planning chart to implement the action steps you will take for each of the next three months.

Month One: Get yourself going. Determine all action steps for months one, two, and three. Make sure that the action steps are easily doable in the first month so that you gain momentum and can have a feeling of success. Set clear criteria for evaluating your progress. Obtain support as needed—an AI buddy, coach, mentor, or therapist. Start taking action right away.

Month Two: Go forward. Continue your commitment to implement your action steps. In working your plan, you may choose to create more action steps as you move forward. Practice your new attitudes and behaviors frequently and repeatedly so that they become familiar new habits. Obtain support as needed—from an AI buddy, coach, mentor, or therapist.

Month Three: Gain momentum, see the goal. Complete the action steps of your plan. Keep in mind the important values you created and visualize the benefits of moving forward with this plan. Obtain support as needed—from an AI buddy, coach, mentor, therapist.

Remember: the AI plan requires you take and complete at least one to three action steps (more if you can be sure you'll follow through) for *each* area of Affluence Intelligence you decided to change. So let's say, for example, you have decided to raise your AI on the priority of peace. You could decide on three action steps you will take each month for three months, such as:

1. Meditation, twenty minutes, Monday, Wednesday, and Friday morning at 8 a.m.
2. Taking a solitary walk on a weekend morning for at least one hour.
3. Read an entertaining magazine or novel at least for one hour, one evening per week.

Take the same approach to doing this as you would in planning a work event or trip. Make the time to sit down and write out the tactical steps necessary to implement your AI plan for each of the next three months. For example, you want to select and meet with a financial advisor. In month one, you will need to talk to people to get referrals (we recommend getting at least three), schedule time to make the phone calls to initiate contact with each of them;

set a deadline by the end of month one for deciding which of the three you will see; and make an appoint to see the advisor in month two. We want you to be very explicit, and write down every step and deadline so that it will happen.

Let's look at Jennifer, a forty-year-old systems analyst who scored particularly low on financial effectiveness and on assertiveness. Jennifer does not like to think or talk about money, but now realizes that this is getting in the way of raising her AI thermostat.

By the end of the three-month plan, Jennifer had made significant progress toward attaining financial effectiveness. As she gained competency she simultaneously gained financial ease. Like learning to swim, when Jennifer jumped into the water of developing financial effectiveness she found that being in the "water" and learning the skills necessary was not as hard as she had anticipated.

SUGGESTED ACTION STEPS

Following are action steps you can take toward changing behaviors, attitudes, and financial effectiveness for each month of the three-month plan. These suggestions will help you decide on the action steps you may choose to take in your personal AI plan. You may find that the suggested steps fit well and work for you, or these suggestions can be a springboard for the creation of your own action steps. But the key is to act!

Month One

Behaviors
Resilience
During the first month:
- Acknowledge your feelings and thoughts about an unresolved situation. As you reflect on these feelings, don't

CHART 11.1 JENNIFER'S THREE-MONTH AFFLUENCE INTELLIGENCE ACTION PLAN

AI Area of Desired Change	Value	Goal	Action Steps Month 1	Action Steps Month 2	Action Steps Month 3	Defenses
Financial competency	I value financial competency in order to have enough money for my needs and wants.	Learn financial basics. Create a budget.	Buy book on financial basics. Commit to an evening class and complete by end of month one. Identify an AI buddy to monitor my progress.	Draft a budget plan: get help as needed. Implement budget: make changes in spending to live within my means.	Meet with a friend or professional advisor to review my budget and consider financial planning for the future.	Procrastination. Spacing out . Telling myself a false story that I am too stupid to understand money.
Financial ease	I value gaining comfort with money in order to have enough money for my needs and wants.	Reduce my anxiety about money. Use my intelligence instead of spacing out or acting dumb about money matters.	Seek money counseling. Plan to have a one hour conversation with my life partner about my money anxiety. Reduce my fear of not knowing my finances by reading my bank and credit card statements. Ask for help as necessary.	Continue to read and review monthly statements.	Talk with at least two of my friends about their ideas and plans in regard money management and retirement.	Procrastination. Spacing out. Telling myself a false story that I am too stupid to understand money.
Assertiveness	I value being more assertive in order to gain a sense of power.	Be assertive at home and at work about money matters.	Prepare to request a raise: practice what I will say to my boss with my AI buddy or friend who is business savvy. Set up a monthly meeting with my partner to discuss finances and retirement.	Set up a meeting with my boss to ask for a raise. Consider other career options: Do a search of jobs available. Gain support from AI buddy and friends.	Follow up on meeting with my boss. If no raise, set up 1 interview with another company. Check in with my AI buddy or friend regarding my progress.	Same as above.

let yourself get stuck in mind-loops of rumination and regret. Use what you have learned to move forward.
- Think of two times in the last sixty days when you felt hurt or angry or upset. Ask yourself, What have I learned from these experiences that will be useful in similar situations in the future?
- Try again at doing one thing that did not go as you had hoped or planned.
- Set deadlines on your calendar to work toward achieving something that you want that you didn't get the first time you tried.

Assertiveness

During the first month:
- Write down the times in your life when you were assertive and it was successful. How did you mobilize yourself? Try it again.
- Write down the times in your life when you were reluctant to be assertive, and write down the defenses you use that created obstacles to asserting yourself.
- Resist the person who is pressuring you to do something you don't want to do. Say, "No, thank you," even if you have to repeat it several times.
- Identify three people you want to say no to, write down what you want to say, and then do it.
- Identify three people you want to say yes to, write down what you want to say, and then do it.

Ability to Work Hard and Achieve Goals

During the first month:
- Write down the top goal(s) you want to achieve.
- Take the one most important goal and write down detailed incremental action steps and a timeline.

- Set goals that are realistic, that you are willing to take action on every day or every week for the next three months. Accountability is more important than your pace or the size of your accomplishment.
- Make a to-do list every night or every morning for one full week. Set priorities and make sure you do your highest priority first.
- Get more organized by taking notes and writing down reminders in your calendar or datebook.

Interpersonal Effectiveness
During the first month:

- Select one person you do not know well. Take him or her out for coffee and keep the conversation focused on learning about them.
- Make it easy for people to tell you what they think by listening well and staying open even if you don't agree with them.
- Share what you have learned in these coffee dates with a friend, AI buddy, or coach.
- Notice when you stop listening, and then get yourself back on track.

Financial Effectiveness

Financial Competence
During the first month:

- Learn the basics of smart personal finance—budgeting, getting out of debt, building savings, investing for retirement, learning how the stock markets work, understanding real estate and alternative investments. You can either:

- › Take a Finance 101 course, either an in-person class or online.
- › Buy and read a comprehensive, accessible book on the topic (examples are Suze Orman's work, or *Personal Finances for Dummies*). See the References and Resources section for more suggestions.

- Identify exactly how much you earn, owe, save, and spend every month.
- Create a monthly budget, putting specific amounts of money in the buckets of earn, spend, save, invest, and share. (It's okay if the amount is $0 in any particular bucket.) You can use an accessible and free resource like Mint.com to organize your budget.
- Make a commitment to living within the means of this budget.
- Get a copy of your credit report.
- Develop a plan to pay off your credit card debt. This plan can include:
  - › Renegotiating the interest rate on your current debt, as well as the interest rate on your current credit card accounts.
  - › Consolidating your debt if it is advantageous for you.
  - › Stopping payment of annual fees on credit cards.
- During the first week of the first month, write down your current needs and wants. Review them with a financial advisor or your Affluence Intelligence buddy.
- Put away your credit card for one month. This will help you see the difference between needs and wants.
- Focus on three areas you need to improve upon. Create doable action steps on issues such as reducing your impulse spending.

Financial Ease

During the first month:

- Write down your attitudes, feelings, and beliefs about earning, saving, investing, spending, and sharing money.
- Write down the answer to the question, What were my family of origin's beliefs, and are my current beliefs the same or different?
- List your current feelings and thoughts about money. For example, think about:
  › If you had no debt, how would you feel?
  › If you spent all of your savings, how would you feel?
  › In what ways do you love or hate money?
  › How does money facilitate or impede your goals?

    Review your answers to determine the steps you need to take in order to gain financial ease. Further your understanding of your thoughts and feelings about money by talking with your AI buddy, trusted friend, or counselor.
- Complete the following sentence: I blame money for. . . . Then ask yourself how this attitude helps you or gets in your way.
- List three skills or financial concepts that you need to learn in order to feel more comfortable and at ease about money.
- Ask yourself the following in order to better understand your emotions about money:
  › How do you feel about friends who have more money than you?
  › How do you feel about friends who have less money than you?
  › Does envy or jealousy get in the way of your relationships? How so?

Take what you have learned to determine the steps you need to take in order to gain financial ease. This may include getting greater understanding of these thoughts and feeling by talking with your AI buddy, trusted friend, or counselor.

Attitudes

Optimism

During the first month:

- Pick one or two areas of your life in which you would like to develop greater optimism (such as relationships, work, finance, and so on). Think about what you do want to have happen, instead of what you don't want to have happen.
- List any strengths you have that will help you become more optimistic in each of these areas.
- Write down what you want for yourself. Read it, say it out loud, and record it. Then review how you sound. Practice saying it until it feels and sounds right.
- Every morning for a month, spend five minutes focusing on having a positive attitude and picturing a positive outcome.

Open-mindedness and Curiosity

During the first month:

- Decide on three situations in which you can explore something new or do something different that is of interest (such as a class, sport, cultural event).
- Notice when you start to judge others in ways that close down opportunities for learning. Stop the judgment, pause, and shift your focus to ask questions to allow you to more fully understand the other person's point of view.

- Observe a very young child and see the world through his or her lens of innocent curiosity.

Ability to Take Control Over Your Life
During the first month:
- Cancel something that you don't want to do.
- Be attentive to a time when you are feeling off center. Take some time off and do something nurturing for yourself.
- Find three opportunities this month to speak up for yourself.
- A friend has asked you to do something. Before you jump to saying yes, pause to make sure you really want to do it.
- When setting a meeting time with a colleague or friend, try stating the time and date that is best for you without hearing from them first.
- Get yourself organized so that you don't waste time redoing work already done or spending time looking for lost documents.

Ambition
During the first month:
- Write down things you like to do with your time or something you would love to achieve, that you never seem to get around to doing. Put a date on your calendar to begin doing what you have chosen to do.
- Remember a time when you were ambitious and felt great. Write down what you did and how you did it. Use this information to guide your next ambition.
- Talk to someone whom you respect who is ambitious and ask him or her to describe how they marshal their energy to be ambitious, as well as what they do to sustain it.
- Pick one small thing you want to get off your to-do list and get it done this week.

- Choose three ambitions that are small enough in scope to begin in month one and achieve by the end of month three. They may be things you enjoy or things that you know you need to do.
- Go see a motivational speaker.

Month Two

Behaviors

Resilience

During the second month:

- Choose a chronic (and perhaps unsolvable) problem or issue that has you feeling depleted, such as dealing with a difficult family member or unpleasant work task, and make a commitment to stop focusing on it for one week.
- If you have a sense of giving up too soon when you hit obstacles, try again or try harder. Stay focused on the possibility of a constructive outcome.
- Don't give up on something that is important for you to accomplish. Keep your eye on the goal; do not be discouraged if the road gets bumpy at times.
- If you believe you have tried repeatedly, discuss with your AI buddy or trusted friend as to what is getting in your way, or whether it is time to stop.

Assertiveness

During the second month:

- Continue to practice saying no. Start with small challenges that are not likely to have big negative consequences.
- Continue to practice saying yes to people who you have wanted to be positive with but have been reluctant to do so.
- When someone asks, What do you want to do?, do not be shy about expressing your point of view.

- Initiate a difficult conversation with someone who matters to you. Communicate what you want clearly. Find a tone of voice that is respectful of yourself and the other person.
- Pick one day every week this month when you are feeling good and be assertive without being aggressive.

Ability to Work Hard and Achieve Goals
During the second month:

- Reward yourself for sticking to what had been in the past a difficult task, such as following your budget or completing onerous paperwork.
- When you are slipping away from your goal, assess the problem and get back on track.
- Pick one more goal you have really wanted to achieve and block off time on your calendar to start doing it this month. Write down detailed incremental action steps and a timeline.
- Push distractions by turning your electronics off, and by setting limits with others requests for your time.

Interpersonal Effectiveness
During the second month:

- Watch yourself: If you are busy seeking approval, you are not being as effective in relationships as you might think.
- Select two more people for a coffee date, with the conversation focused on learning about their lives.
- Learn and practice the Non-Violent Communication Method developed by Marshall Rosenberg (www.nvc.org), a communication strategy that can help you clarify your needs and feelings, and communicate in effective ways.
- Pick one day this month to make a favorable impression by putting your best foot forward to those you come in contact with.

- Take note of how you feel in different situations, notice when you are comfortable and when you are not comfortable. Become aware of how much of the discomfort is located in you, the other person, or the situation. Use this information to guide what you may or may not say or do in the future.

Financial Effectiveness

Financial Competence

During the second month:

- Continue learning about your finances. Review your credit card statement, bank statements, and brokerage statements. Continue the focus on the three areas you need to improve upon, as determined in month one.
- Learn about your tax bracket, and how you can make financial decisions that work for you.
- Create a rainy day savings account for emergency backup; fund it with a minimum amount every month.
- Choose one incentive to help you to start to save (such as saving for a need or a want).
- Choose one area of your spending to reduce debt. Consider reducing or ending your spending on items that are wants rather than needs (such as gourmet coffee, retail therapy to cheer you up, or eating out).
- Balance your checkbooks.
- If you are over thirty years old, start a retirement account (no matter how small) and fund it every month.

Financial Ease

During the second month:

- Start a financial ease journal in which you write down specific situations or experiences you have had that trigger discomfort, as well as situations or experiences with money in which you felt particularly at ease. Describe the trigger situation (including whom you were with) and the feelings or thoughts that arose.

- Have a conversation with two different friends about your work on developing financial ease. Find out (and write down) what they do to exercise financial ease.
- Find a book, class, or mentor to learn the skills necessary to make you feel more financially effective. Ask your friends and colleagues for recommendations. Search the web for local resources.

Attitudes

Optimism

During the second month:

- Think of three attitudes or feelings you want to have in your life and state them as if you already have them. For example, instead of saying, "I want to feel content," say, "I feel content."
- Start a journal of optimism in which you list new experiences you want to have and that will give you a chance to be optimistic.
- When you start to feel cynical or find yourself engaging in negative self-talk, realize that you have a choice about your attitude toward any situation, and that having a negative attitude will likely lead to a more negative outcome.
- Practice shifting from an attitude of scarcity to that of abundance. If you are thinking about a particular challenge from a "cup half empty" perspective, pause and shift to a "cup half full" perspective.
- Review your work on exercising optimism with your AI buddy or trusted friend.

Open-mindedness and Curiosity

During the second month:

- Cultivate curiosity. Start conversations with others by asking about what is new or important in their lives. Keep the focus of these conversations more on learning about their lives than talking about yours. Ask questions such as, "Can you tell me more about that? What was that like for you? Is there anything else that is new or important that you might want to talk about?" Find someone whose lifestyle is very different from your own. This can be a neighbor, shopkeeper, Pilates teacher, or anyone whose chosen path is not a mirror image of yours. Learn about their life so you can retell their story—their challenges, hopes, joys, and sorrows. Think of yourself as an investigative reporter who really wants to learn about the other person's story, to get the important emotional and situational details that bring the story to life.
- Review your work on exercising greater open-mindedness and curiosity with your AI buddy or trusted friend.

Ability to Take Control Over Your Life

During the second month:

- Make a list of the items in your life that you can control and need to take action on. Starting with the easiest item, tackle one per week.
- Make a list of times in your current life that leave you feeling out of control. With this recognition, work on taking hold of your emotions or enlist someone to help you with your emotions. (See next recommendation.)
- Be attentive to when you have emotions that make you feel overly vulnerable or out of control. When you notice these feelings, then:

> Give yourself a "time out" to get centered and balanced.
> Remind yourself of a time and situation in which you felt centered, in charge, and calm.

- Remember times when your self-esteem and sense of personal power were strong and balanced. Write down these memories, and keep them available as a tool to help you regain control and balance when you have received a blow to your self-esteem.

- If you notice that you are expending psychic energy worrying about something that you already know is futile, take control by:
  > Changing your psychological channel: make a concerted effort to focus on a different issue, one in which you feel in charge.
  > If there is nothing more to learn from your worrying, then work on letting go/grieving over it to attain a renewed sense of control. Remember the stages of grieving are denial, anger, bargaining, depression, and acceptance. If necessary, talk with your AI buddy, or seek professional help.

Ambition

During the second month:

- Find an AI buddy, coach, or mentor to help motivate you.
- Do the work necessary to exercise the three small ambitions you set in month one.
- Decide on a domain of focused pursuit (such as improving your work performance, practicing a more difficult song on the guitar, exercising more, or improving your tennis game) for months two and three, or a single ambitious pursuit for months two and three.

- Choose one small thing you would really enjoy doing, and start doing it this month.

Month Three

Behaviors

Resilience

During the third month:

- Continue action steps from months one and two.
- Consider an action step that is out of your comfort zone that would push your capacity for resilience.
- Stop ruminating on a chronic problem(s) that leaves you feeling depleted or upset. Tell yourself: I've given this issue more than sufficient thought, and have taken whatever actions I can take at this time. My ruminations needlessly burn psychic energy—like being in a car that is endlessly sitting at a stop sign with the engine running. So I will put this matter to rest, accepting that I have done my best. I will focus on finding more constructive ways to use my energy.
- What do you need to do to make a change that you have already decided to make? Stop thinking about it. Go ahead and do it! If, for example, you're getting over the end of a relationship, and you feel ready to start dating, take small steps to explore opportunities for a new relationship, such as creating an online dating profile, and letting a few people know that you are looking.

Assertiveness

During the third month:

- Plan a day just for you to do what you really want to do.
- Continue to set limits with others to minimize your frustration.

- Assert a positive intention or response at least three times this month.
- Choose two things that you have wanted or needed to get done and make sure you complete the task.

Ability to Work Hard and Achieve Goals

During the third month:

- One day each week, pick two or three small tasks that you need or want to get done and do them before you do anything else.
- Pick one thing this month that you will really enjoy achieving and put it on the calendar.
- Give yourself five minutes each week to reflect on the things you have accomplished and feel the satisfaction that comes with accomplishment.

Interpersonal Effectiveness

During the third month:

- Notice yourself—such as your body language and your opening line—when you first greet someone. Given what you have noticed, would you be more effective by altering your style? If so, experiment with different ways of greeting people.
- As an interaction with another person unfolds, notice when you begin to make judgments—about yourself or the other person—as they can get in the way of effectively listening to the other person.
- Practice the art of disagreeing in a respectful manner.
- Talk with someone who is completely different from you and be curious and interested rather than judging his or her differences.

Financial Effectiveness

Financial Competence

During the third month:

- Set up a meeting with a financial advisor or tax accountant to go over your finances.
- Start an account for "rainy days" and/or for "fun days."
- Review your insurance premiums to make sure they cover your needs. Do some comparison shopping between insurance companies.
- Review your financial plan, including how you want to pass on assets in your estate. For example, people can develop a simple estate plan and avoid probate by creating a living trust. If your trust is not up to date, schedule an appointment with your advisor.
- Review your charitable giving. Align your giving with your values, and importantly, your financial situation.

Financial Ease

During the third month:

- Review your financial ease journal on a weekly basis. Think about how you could gain greater financial ease by a change in your attitude or behavior. For example, imagine you are eating lunch with people who started talking about "market volatility." You start to feel uncomfortable because you do not understand what they are talking about. Next time, instead of withdrawing from the conversation and feeling stupid, ask your friends to explain what they mean by market volatility.
- Take someone out to lunch or let them take you out for lunch. Notice the differences in your feelings. How does it feel? Are you more or less comfortable being in the giving

or receiving role? If this exercise has identified issues that get in the way of attaining financial ease, then create action steps that will change your attitudes or behaviors as necessary.

- If you are a saver, say yes to giving yourself a treat. If you are a spender, say no to the very thing you want to buy this week.
- Continue learning, talking, and reading about the world of money and personal finance.

Attitudes

Optimism

During the third month:

- Continue action steps from months one and two that you found particularly helpful.
- Don't take yourself so seriously for one day this month.
- Think of a difficult situation. Ask yourself, What did I learn? Avoid asking, Whom can I blame?
- Talk with some optimists and see how you feel when you are with them.
- Listen and look for opportunities! These can only be seen through an optimistic lens.

Open-mindedness and Curiosity

During the third month:

- Have a conversation with a person who you know has opposing thoughts or beliefs about a particular topic. Your goal is to fully understand their perspective.
- Go to a talk or form of entertainment that you would ordinarily avoid.
- Go to a family member or close friend and ask, "Is there something important about yourself that you would like me to know?"

- At a social engagement, talk to someone you know little about and be curious about his or her life. Ask questions, and listen more than talk.

Ability to Take Control Over Your Life
During the third month:
- Before you make a decision, take the time to think it through, even if that means having to call someone back later.
- Let people know, given your schedule, when it is best for you to receive phone calls.
- When the details of life leave you feeling out of control, pause and review your priorities and values.
- Take one area of your life that is stressful for you and that you can do something about, and focus on that one item without procrastination.
- Choose one thing you have always wanted to do and just go for it!
- Choose one thing you have always wanted to stop doing and just stop doing it!
- Ask yourself when things do not go well: What have I contributed to this situation or outcome? In taking responsibility for my part, what could I do differently in the future?

Ambition
During the third month:
- Do one task that you previously either avoided or put off. Once completed, give yourself a treat or reward.
- Fill in the following statement: I will make the commitment and take action to do _____ this month.
- Fill in the following: I will overcome _____ that gets in my way of moving forward this month.

Every Month

Behaviors

Resilience

Every month:

- Observe yourself and ask: what attitudes and behaviors are getting in my way?
- Be mindful of the ways in which you engage in negative internal conversations with yourself ("negative self-talk"), such as telling yourself that there must be something wrong with you, or that you will never get over not getting the promotion you sorely wanted, the house that you couldn't quite afford, or a more successful or easier going life partner. As you practice this self-awareness, see how you can refocus your energy on what you can do or accomplish.
- Disrupt the automatic pilot of self-negation or self-excuse by creating a pause in your inner narrative. Imagine you were touching the "hold" button on a telephone conversation. In that pause:
  › Take command of your inner voice to replace negative self-talk with positive self-talk.
  › Remind yourself of your strengths and accomplishments.
  › Tell yourself there will be other opportunities.
  › Don't get stuck in the present. Tell yourself that things will look different tomorrow.
- Acknowledge all positive outcomes, no matter how small.

Assertiveness

Every month:

- When talking, practice ending your sentences as statements, rather than letting your voice rise as if you were asking a question.

- Watch your body language: Stand up straight and look the other person in the eye.
- Don't apologize when you have done nothing wrong.
- Watch out for your "automatic smile" response to conflict. If this is your predisposition, increase your awareness of how and when you smile.
- The next time you are interrupted, let the talker know that you have not yet finished speaking.
- Communicate your intentions clearly.
- Don't overextend yourself on a regular basis.

Ability to Work Hard and Achieve Goals
Every month:
- Use an AI buddy, engage a mentor, or get support from a valued friend or colleague to keep you moving forward on your journey to affluence.
- Start a habit of making a morning or evening to-do list and identify priorities to keep in mind for the day.
- Set aside a minimum of two hours of uninterrupted time to get one important task done.
- Stay mindful of your most highly valued goals.
- Set realistic goals for yourself so they can be attained.

Interpersonal Effectiveness
Every month:
- Ask questions for clarification.
- Maintain your point of view even if others don't agree with you.
- Validate your own thoughts and feelings.
- Validate the thoughts and feelings of another person.

- Regulate your emotions, even when others are upset or overly emotional. Use a tone of voice that reflects your capacity to control your emotions.
- Stay mindful of your behavior: Are you relating to others in an open and relaxed way?
- Listen to the cues of those you are talking to and react or respond appropriately.

Financial Effectiveness

Financial Competence

Every month:

- Open and carefully review your bank and credit card statements. If you don't understand them, call your AI buddy, friend, or advisor.
- Take thirty minutes to think about what you need for retirement.
- Give up at least one thing that you spend money on and put that amount in a savings account or investment account.
- Practice pausing before you spend money on your wants, and make sure that spending fits your values and your plan before you make the purchase.

Financial Ease

Every month:

- On Monday of each week of your three-month plan, list the emotions or thoughts you have about yourself when it comes to one of the following money-related activities:
  - › Earning
  - › Investing
  - › Saving
  - › Spending
  - › Sharing

- Ask yourself each week if your emotions or thoughts are moving you in the direction you want to go. If the answer is no, then start to imagine what you would need to think or feel in order to change that.
- Notice the judgments you make about your friends and colleagues when it comes to consumption: clothes, homes, cars, toys, and vacations. Notice how these judgments about yourself or others result in discomfort.
- Read articles about money and finance in areas that you need and want more financial ease.

Attitudes

Optimism

Every month:

- At the beginning of each week, let yourself believe that what you think is impossible is actually possible.
- Imagine future scenarios that turn out well.
- In meeting a challenge, practice believing you can handle it and get through the challenge.
- When you are in doubt, think "yes"; move the feeling and thought of "no" aside.
- Listen closely inside yourself for the voice of defeat. As soon as you notice this voice, try to stop that voice and talk yourself back into a better frame of mind.

Open-mindedness and Curiosity

Every month:

- Practice "beginner's mind," in which you approach a person or topic as if you were learning about it for the first time, with a fresh attitude and open heart.
- Always ask yourself, especially when things go wrong: what can I learn from this situation?

- If you find that your mind is closed, pause for a moment and try your best to find something of interest or of value in the other perspective. Imagine you had to take the position of the other, and argue that point of view.

Ability to Take Control Over Your Life
Every month:
- Don't be quick to give away your rights or power.
- Pay attention to your thoughts and feelings when you start to feel out of control. Find the trigger point that shifts you from your baseline to feeling off center or not in charge of yourself. Use what you have learned to increase your awareness of when you are triggered, so you can pause and step back, and take action to regain control and balance.
- When others make a request, don't say yes too quickly. Tell the person making the request that you have to think about it and will let them know your answer shortly.
- If you determine that a conflict must be addressed, then confront others about their role in the problematic situation. While this may be initially difficult, it will help you feel more in control.
- Don't feel you have to defend yourself or give reasons as to why you can't or don't want to do something.
- Delegate some of your workload.
- Set goals that are doable: If you over- or underestimate the time that it takes to attain your goals, then either change your goals or determine actions you need to take, such as change of goals, time frames, attitudes, and/or behaviors.
- Protect your personal and social obligations just as you do your business obligations by putting them on the calendar and following through.

Ambition

Every month:

- Because self-esteem is important when it comes to ambition, acknowledge compliments from others, and also compliment yourself.
- Stop doing things that get in the way of your focused pursuit.
- Notice when you start to procrastinate, and ask yourself what your procrastination is about. Give yourself credit for noticing without judgment.
- Stop making comparisons. Remind yourself that making comparisons is not useful and can often get in the way of moving forward.
- Don't back away in the face of criticism or discomfort.
- Watch your mindset! You don't have to feel ambitious to be ambitious.
- Take on a volunteer project. This can include projects such as coaching a children's sports team, doing an art project, volunteering for an independent project at school or work, and so on.

COMPLETION OF THE AI
THREE-MONTH PLAN: TAKING STOCK

If you have followed through on your three-month plan and done your best to attain your goals, then congratulations! You have taken the most critical step in raising your Affluence Intelligence—you have empowered yourself to be the key change agent of your life, to be the leader that you need to follow!

Now it is time to take stock of what you have accomplished, and what you want to continue to work on, or new attitudes and behaviors you want to live by. Look at what you have accomplished: Make a list of the progress you have made on each of the goals you have set for yourself. Take notice of your success in moving forward, however small the steps, even the times when you had to pause or circle back. Take pride in having started the process of changing attitudes and behaviors. Remember that when patterns have been set for a long time, change is challenging: It is often the tortoise rather than the hare that wins this race.

Next, look at the obstacles that impeded your progress on specific goals. For each goal you have set:

1. List the action steps that you did not complete or found to be difficult.
2. For each of these action steps, take note of:
    a. the external factors—the behavior of other people, the state of the economy—that got in your way.
    b. the internal factors—your defenses—that got in your way.

We have complete confidence that you can raise your AI thermostat if you have worked your plan in a serious, deliberate, and persistent way. If you have found that you did not want to put in the necessary planning and effort, then we suggest you choose the path of acceptance, and find personal power and peace in accepting exactly who you are and what you are willing (or not willing) to do at this stage of your life.

chapter twelve

AT THE HEART OF AFFLUENCE

Tim was a middle manager for a manufacturing company in Texas. He was a well-respected employee both by those above and below him. Tim worked hard at his job—he didn't get home most days until 7:30 p.m., and he worked most Saturdays. He was doing very well, and intended to buy a new car and a fishing boat. But in 2008 his company was acquired by a multinational. In 2009, during the heat of the financial downturn, management decided to downsize his department, laying off most of the employees, including Tim.

Tim was stunned. After fifteen years of employment and a golden record, his company had given him three months' severance and three days to clear his desk. He immediately began a job search, but found nothing available.

We know that our message of thinking big, living your priorities, and trying to achieve affluence may be harder to accept in these difficult times. People are out of work; homes are in foreclosure. People have told us that they have had to learn to move beyond their anxiety about not having money, and push themselves to look at a different side of themselves. They have had to learn to live in a different way. For some, this new life has turned out to be more satisfying than their previous life.

During this difficult period, Tim and his wife reviewed their values. The time off work forced him to look long and hard at what really mattered. They rethought their future as if they were starting life all over again. It was surprisingly easy to know: their priorities were peace and productivity (work) to provide for financial security, not a pot of gold, or more Power. They wanted life in a small to medium-size town, where they knew their neighbors. They wanted a place with decent public schools. They wanted to be within a two-hour drive of their closest relatives. They wanted to live within their means, and stop using credit cards. They wanted a great place to enjoy raising their daughter. They also wanted to live near the mountains, for as Tim said, "I am deeply satisfied when we're camping or walking in the mountains."

Tim changed his job search tactics. He began to look for where he *wanted to* live, rather than for where a job happened to be. He identified six places in the Mountain States. On a visit to a school in one of these towns, Tim noticed a low-level management job on a bulletin board. He applied and got the job. His wife's work as a nurse was "portable"—she started working in a local hospital. They were making less money, but Tim was home for dinner almost every night, he had his weekends for himself and his family, and he was living within a half-hour drive of the mountains he loved. Tim also started a part-time consulting business, in which his skills at financial management could be helpful to businesses in transition.

For Tim and his family there was an unexpected benefit of this economic catastrophe. He began to drive his life by his core values, rather than by the career ladder of a company. He let go of the relentless "More! More! More!" that characterizes our culture of consumption. He understood that the quality of his time was fundamental to being truly affluent. So he and his wife made a lifestyle choice in which the amount of money for their needs and wants was directly related to how they wanted to spend their time and raise their daughter. As we have seen hundreds of times leading retreats and family meetings, when your financial life is driven by your core values, and you are willing to work hard and persevere, then chances for success are very high.

We believe it is vital for each of us to gain a deep and abiding trust in our capacities to do what needs to be done. You liberate yourself when you take responsibility for your life and say, "I am going to take myself seriously and I am going to make my life better. I understand that I have the capacity to make important and essential changes in my life, and I am willing to make a solemn commitment. I have faith in my ability to do the work that is required of me, and to meet my commitments every day. I will expand my horizons and do far more than I had ever thought possible." For some, like Tim, this commitment may be to take on a philosophy of "less is more," to simplify life, and to deepen the experience of what they love. For others, it may mean moving from less *to* more, expanding horizons to create a life that is aligned with their most important priorities.

In the last few chapters, we've been focused on the details of how you unlock your Affluence Intelligence. Now we want you to step back and look at the big picture of what affluence can mean in your life. Time and time again, we have seen our clients transform themselves. It's true that when they have increased their AIQs they have made more money, but they also have better relationships, less anxiety, improved health, and a greater sense of joy and possibility. Simply put, you can have a better life, no matter what your skills and strengths, or whatever your challenges and vulnerabilities.

Taking the test and getting your scores was the first step in this journey. Our wish for you is that you will follow through and make the necessary changes, so you can open your eyes to what is possible for you. Take a moment to congratulate yourself on being smart enough to see that your life can be better, and brave enough to take stock of yourself as objectively as you can.

Unlocking Affluence Intelligence means turning the key and opening the door to having freedom—to having a sense of choice and control to create a life that reflects what matters most to you. As you open the door, you will begin to see yourself with a new honesty and clarity. Maybe it won't be a perfect version of life as you thought it was going to be, but it can certainly be more affluent than it is today. It will be a life in which your actions are better aligned with your intentions, a life in which you are driven by the forces within you that give you personal meaning, purpose, and power.

You may wonder, "Will following this plan make me rich? Will I have more money at the end of this journey?" We can say without a doubt that if you follow the program, you will feel much happier and live life with an attitude of abundance. You may very well have more money. But at the end of the day, as Charlene puts it, the number of zeros in your bank account won't buy you self-esteem, love, or gratitude. (Remember, of the five Affluence Intelligence priorities, only one concerns money.) As you tap into your Affluence Intelligence, you will exercise the muscles needed to gain what we call "financial satisfaction"—a life that finds harmony between money and personal fulfillment.

This is the historical moment to discover and leverage your Affluence Intelligence. The aftermath of the Great Recession has been a wake-up call for all of us, a time for the rethinking of what really matters—not just for the banking industry, but for how each of us thinks about and plans for our daily lives. We have all seen the havoc created when large institutions overly focus on "the money of the moment," losing track of their raison d'être, forgetting the bigger picture. Indeed, for some of these companies, their loss of perspective has meant their demise, ultimately having a powerful impact on most people around the globe. This same phenomenon happens to individuals, when they let a fraction of what is important define the whole, when they lose perspective of who they are and what makes them happy. Now, more than ever, each of us needs to take the opportunity to reprioritize, to maximize our strengths, and to build joyous and satisfying lives. It is time for all of us to take a serious look at the types of choices we make and goals we set, so that we can achieve an optimal balance of self, family, and social satisfaction that meets our deepest needs and wants.

Beyond luck and timing, what enabled our clients to become wealthy, and then to sustain it? Without a doubt, our clients have shown us that it was always more than an obsession with having a lot of money that led to their success. They did exactly what we've been talking about in this book; they had the desire and real commitment to be engaged with what truly matters to them, and to use the appropriate AI attitudes and behaviors necessary to make choices that provided them with personal and financial satisfaction. Listen to George, a sixty-year-old self-made millionaire in real estate construction, answer his adult children's question, What made you so successful? What did you do that others do not?

He responded,

> I'm so grateful for our good fortune. There are many people who worked as hard and as long as we did and did not get the big payoff. But I woke up excited and ready every day I got up to go to work. Time flew by. We put together a management team. Really, the whole company worked as a team—that gave their all. Everyone offered to do what they did well, and were never hesitant to run the extra mile when needed. Every day we focused on working hard, doing our best, having integrity, and having a great time. We had fun together. We took care of each other. Yes, we were good at marketing our know-how, and we were lucky to be in a part of the country that was on the economic upswing. Of course we wanted to be profitable. But we built this business on our abilities, not on meeting a particular economic goal. We listened well to the feedback our clients gave. We made sure they were satisfied. I can honestly say that I would be very happy today even if we hadn't struck gold. Some of the best days I will always remember were in the first few years, when we were struggling. We had to make daily decisions as to how to maximize our efforts, and reduce risks to survive. All my life I have found that when I follow my interests and abilities, I have been successful. And that is what I wish for all of my children.

As in George's story, if you were to follow affluent people as they go through an average day, you would see that they are acutely aware of how they spend their time, and that they enjoy taking risks that challenge them but do not push them to live outside of their means. These are people who are assertive and careful, fun and focused, leaders who love to build teams, people who enjoy giving back. Like all of us, they have vulnerabilities and shortcomings. But they are not ashamed to acknowledge them; they work around them, or they are open to learning from them.

No matter how large or small your pocketbook, life is a rollercoaster ride. You want the best ride possible. For some this comes naturally, but most of us have to stay aware and work at keeping our attitudes and actions in synch with our goals. This does not mean being like the people we read about in *The Millionaire Next Door*, people who simply save their pennies for a rainy day, taking the most conservative route to wealth. Rather, it's about people staying focused on the big picture—where you are going in your life—and at the same time enjoying the process. Keep your eye on the goal. This will give you perspective—a way of being engaged, but not enveloped, by a relationship, business, or activity. Live your life being aware that this is the only one you will ever have.

If you are completely content with your life, that's wonderful. But if you feel that something is missing or that other people have something you don't have, and you want to learn from people who live rich and fulfilling lives, then make a commitment to using these strategies.

We believe that those with Affluence Intelligence share a perspective on life similar to those who are on a serious spiritual path: They are wholly engaged in life, but do not identify with any one single particular aspect of it. In the chapter on resetting your Affluence Factor thermostat, we talked about the defense of "grasping." This involves a psychological attachment that is so pursued, valued, and tightly held that a disappointment can result in feeling a loss of oneself, like a life-ending tragedy. When we are entrapped by this kind of disappointment, we need to be able to step back from feeling that all is lost and regain perspective. Here it is useful to exercise the capacity for *merging*. This capacity (available in all of us) provides for that special tender closeness in love, and requires "merging without merging," which means being able to be very close without the loss of one's personal boundaries and selfhood.[1]

So it is with success. As you pursue your goals with passion and perseverance, know that the process itself is a payoff. In the practice of meditation, it is the experience of the "mind watching the mind," not the attainment of realization or Nirvana (which may only come in fleeting moments), that is the core of spiritual work. Similarly, if you engage in practicing your AI action plan consistently (realize that there will be good days and bad days), you will achieve success. The ultimate goal is to attain inner freedom, a sense of security and empowerment, the ability to see the array of choices that are available to you, and be able to rally your resources to respond effectively to external circumstances, both within and beyond your control.

Like any program that you undertake to improve yourself, whether it is a diet, exercise regimen, or life-strategy plan, you will only succeed if your efforts are sustained. We encourage you to have a new bottom line, a new foundation for what you expect and can get from life. Make it real by committing to your Affluence Intelligence program of sustainability. If you want Affluence Intelligence, then you need to get fully on board. This means making the commitment to focus, follow through, and have faith in the process. As one of our clients is fond of saying, you have to: "Do what you say and say what you do."

You must ignore the negative internal voice that tells you that you do not have it in you to succeed, and instead listen to the voice that wants what is best for you, that wants you to be affluent. You must work toward the money, focusing on what matters most, following through on your commitments, and managing your defenses in ways that help rather than hinder your progress. For some it will take doing hard work, while for others it can be as simple as saying "no" on a daily basis to what is holding you back and saying "yes" to what is right for you. This means no more excuses—you maintain a deep and unwavering belief in yourself and in the process. Take the leap.

Finally, while having enough money for your needs and wants is important, we believe that people's lives should not be primarily governed by money. In fact, people who make money their central value typically neither preserve their wealth nor their family unity. These are the families that will suffer from the three-generation wealth phenomenon: in more than 80 percent of cases, the wealth created will be gone by the end of the third generation.

Are some of the wealthy into their money for the power, for the influence it offers? Yes, absolutely. But when power is what drives someone to acquire wealth, the payoff is limited, and may not result in deep, sustainable personal satisfaction. We've all heard the stories of the lonely rich person, living in a home that is nothing more than a gilded cage. They leave home only to shop and acquire more than they'll ever need. They find themselves in a world of people they can't trust, or "friends" that they have bought. Lacking a sense of meaning and purpose, not having joy in their relationships, they go through life feeling ill at ease with themselves and looking for the next distraction to fill in the void. Our client Max, for example, was extremely afraid of people finding out that he had inherited millions of dollars. He lived in a small northwestern town in an upper middle class home. He was obsessed with the fear of how his money would lead him to be exploited, hurt, or physically injured. So he hunkered down and pretended to not have money.

His escape valve was occasional trips to Manhattan, staying at the Four Seasons for a week or two, spending freely (he had only acquaintances, not close friends in New York City), and then returning to his withdrawn existence.

This is not living a life of affluence. This is being rich, lonely, and depressed. Increasing your Affluence Intelligence allows you more joy and satisfaction, in yourself, with the people you love, and in your community. You, like Howard or Charlene, Amy or David, can be leaders and team players, valued members of their communities. Max's story, and the story of the many people we have encountered where big money only meant big problems, led us to create the Money, Meaning & Choices Institute. But it was people whose stories were filled with triumph, passion, and optimism that led us to write this book. It was from these American success stories that we learned the importance of living all seven elements of Affluence Intelligence. No one element trumps the others, including having money.

We have dedicated our professional careers to helping people live better lives. And we want you to live a better life, too. Spending time talking to people who have become very rich, who also manage to have personal integrity, to truly invest in their important relationships, and are concerned about how they can best improve the lives of others, has been inspiring to us. What is perhaps most inspiring is that they are really just like us—not some different, rare breed, or blue blooded, wildly smart, or gorgeous. What makes these very wealthy and successful people different from the rest of us? The answer is that they believed that they could change the stories of their lives. Not perfectly, and not always with the best timing. And certainly not without detours and bumps in the road. But they believed that being affluent was possible, and that they had the power within, to stay focused and find the resources in the world around themselves to make that happen. Just as that is possible for you.

Being affluent is within your grasp. Visualize having the keys in your hand, watching yourself put the key inside the lock, hearing the tumblers turn, and the lock click open. Now feel the key in your pocket, waiting for your initiative and courage to use it to start the journey. Let the Affluence Intelligence keys unlock the power that is already inside you, taking you to a place of greater personal and financial wealth.

Keys for unlocking your Affluence Intelligence:

- ✓ Adjust your attitude: make the commitment, do the work.
- ✓ Keep the faith: believe in yourself, believe in your goals.
- ✓ The process is the product: the journey toward the goal is as satisfying (if not more so) as getting to the goal itself.
- ✓ There's a price and a payoff for your choices: create a life with little regret.
- ✓ Stop moving without thinking: identify what really matters to you. Remind yourself daily.
- ✓ You are the builder, the creator of your future: don't let the future be overly defined by the past.
- ✓ Keep perspective: don't define the whole of your happiness by any one fraction.
- ✓ Start small: just getting started is a success in itself.
- ✓ Remember that financial worth is not equal to self-worth.

Unlock your Affluence Intelligence, and live a life that best reflects who you really are.

NOTES

CHAPTER 4

1. www.authentichappiness.sas.upenn.edu/Default.aspx.

2. S. Goldbart, D. T. Jaffe, & J. DiFuria, "Money, meaning, and identity: Coming to terms with being wealthy," in T. Kasser and A. D. Kanner (Eds.). *Psychology and consumer culture: The struggle for a good life in a materialistic world* (Washington, DC: American Psychological Association, 2003).

CHAPTER 6

1. Institute for Women's Policy Research (IWPR) Fact Sheet, The Gender Wage Gap: 2010, IWPR #C350, updated April 2011. Available at www.iwpr.org/publications/by-date.

2. A. T. Lo Sasso, M. R. Richards, et al., "The $16,819 Pay Gap for Newly Trained Physicians: The Unexplained Trend of Men Earning More Than Women," *Health Affairs* 30(2) (February 2011), 193–201.

3. There are many people who have chosen to give their wealth away during their lifetime. For example, Warren Buffet has given most of his assets to the Gates Foundation. Look at the stories found in the book, *We Gave Away a Fortune,* by Chris Mogil and Ann Slepian.

4. The baby boomers' lack of planning was supported by economic policies and politics that moved away from traditional American values, which embraced spending, to values that pressed for unchecked consumption in a very media-driven marketplace. Never has such a large cohort of society been so pressured to use credit and live beyond their means. Now, and looking forward, the boomers are in big financial trouble. While the American economic policy and the mass media

231

may have fanned the flames of their spending, it has, since the 1980s, been slowly but surely demolishing their financial safety net.

5. Msmoney.com: "The Financial Basics." www.msmoney.com/mm /get_started/get_started/index.htm; SuzyOrman.com: "Resource Center." www.suzeorman.com; Knight Kiplinger: "Eight Keys to Financial Security." www.kiplinger.com; Joline Godfrey, Raising Financially Fit Kids.

CHAPTER 8

1. Hank Vyner, personal communication with authors, 2011.

2. For more detail on this topic see Goldbart and Wallin's book, *Mapping the Terrain of the Heart: Passion, Tenderness, and the Capacity for Love.*

CHAPTER 10

1. All of the charts in this book are available as PDF downloads for readers on our website, www.affluenceintelligence.com.

CHAPTER 12

1. Goldbart and Wallin, *Mapping the Terrain of the Heart*, ch. 2, "The Capacity for Merging: The role of boundaries in love."

RESOURCES AND REFERENCES

Here is a list of references cited in this book as well as books, web sites, and organizations that can be helpful on your journey toward Affluence Intelligence.

MONEY AND WEALTH PSYCHOLOGY

Brickman, Philip, and Donald Campbell. "Hedonic Relativism and Planning the Good Society." In Apley, M. H. (Ed.). *Adaptation Level Theory: A Symposium.* Academic Press, 1971.

DiFuria, Joan, M.A., Stephen Goldbart, Ph.D., and Dennis T. Jaffe, Ph.D. 2002. Money, Meaning & Choices Institute Monographs. Kentfield, CA: Money, Meaning & Choices Institute. Available at www.mmcinstitute.com. Titles include:

- *Family Meetings about Money: Holding Successful Discussions about Sensitive Topics.* (This booklet is particularly helpful as many of the family meeting resource materials are targeted for families with closely held businesses, where this is for all families.)
- *Governing Wealth Across the Generations*
- *Money and Children*
- *Using Wealth Wisely: Questions and Answers about Money, Relationships and Inheritance*
- *Your Money and Your Life: Money Preference Guide*

Gilbert, Daniel. *Stumbling on Happiness.* Knopf, 2006.

Goldbart, S., D. T. Jaffe, and J. DiFuria. "Money, meaning, and identity: Coming to terms with being wealthy." In: Kasser, T., and A. D. Kanner (Eds.). *Psychology and Consumer Culture: The Struggle for a Good Life in a Materialistic World.* American Psychological Association, 2003.

Hughes, Jay, Jr. *Family: The Compact Among Generations.* Bloomberg Books, 2007.

Kahneman, Daniel, and Angus Deaton. "High income improves evaluation of life but not emotional well-being." *Proceedings of the National Academy of Sciences (PNAS)* 107, no. 38 (September 21, 2010): 16489–16493.

Lo Sasso, A. T., M. R. Richards, et al., "The $16,819 Pay Gap for Newly Trained Physicians: The Unexplained Trend of Men Earning More Than Women," *Health Affairs* 30, no. 2 (February, 2011), 193–201.

Perle, Liz. *Money, A Memoir.* Henry Holt & Co., 2006.

Schervish, Paul and Keith Whitaker. *Wealth and the Will of God: Discerning the Use of Riches in the Service of Ultimate Purpose.* Indiana University Press, 2010.

Stanley, Thomas, and William Danko. *The Millionaire Next Door: Surprising Secrets of America's Wealthy.* Pocket Books, 1996.

POSITIVE PSYCHOLOGY AND BRAIN PLASTICITY

Cohen, Gene. *The Mature Mind: The Positive Power of the Aging Brain.* Basic Books, 2006.

Csikszentmihalyi, Mihaly. *Flow: The Psychology of Optimal Experience.* Harper Perennial, 1991.

Goldbart, Stephen, Ph.D., and David Wallin, Ph.D. *Mapping the Terrain of the Heart: Passion, Tenderness, and the Capacity for Love.* Jason Aronson, 1996.

Goleman, Daniel. *Emotional Intelligence.* Bantam Books, 1995.

Kübler-Ross, E. *On Grief and Grieving: Finding the Meaning of Grief Through the Five Stages of Loss.* Simon & Schuster, 2005.

Lyubomirsky, Sonja, Ph.D. *The How of Happiness: A Scientific Approach to Getting the Life YOU Want.* Penguin Press, 2007. The concept of the "happiness set point" was coined by Dr. Lyubomirsky.

Rosenberg, Marshall, Ph.D. *Nonviolent Communication: A Language of Life.* 2nd ed. Puddledancer Press, 2003.

Seligman, Martin, with Christopher Peterson. *Character Strengths and Virtues, A Handbook and Classification.* Oxford University Press, 2004. This is a landmark tome offering a classification system for positive psychology diagnostics. Dr. Martin Seligman is also the director of a major national resource on positive psychology, The Positive Psychology Center, University of Pennsylvania (http://www.ppc.sas.upenn.edu).

Siegel, Dan. *Mindsight: The New Science of Transformation.* Random House, 2010.

Suzuki, S. *Zen Mind, Beginner's Mind.* Shambala, 2011.

FINANCIAL COMPETENCY & EDUCATION-TACTICAL TOOLS

Investing Pays Off: http://philanthropy.ml.com/ipo/. Financial competency curriculum that can be used by volunteers in the classroom or by parents at home. Designed in three levels from ages 7 to 18. Print materials (at no charge) directly from the web site. Easy to use, with minimal preparation time; lessons and worksheets are all prepared. Materials aim to prepare young people for tomorrow by arming them with the knowledge and know-how essential for financial and career success.

Knight Kiplinger. Eight Keys to Financial Security. www.kiplinger.com.

Lightbulb Press Guides: www.lightbulbpress.com. Lightbulb guides clearly explain important financial concepts, such as investing, using credit, financial planning, and retirement. Guides are filled with helpful illustrations, fascinating sidebars, and real-world examples to help drive home key lessons, and to keep readers engaged.

Money Savvy Kids: www.moneysavvykids.com. Order the four-slotted piggy bank to teach concepts of money management including: save, spend, donate, and invest. (Bank $14.95, supplemental materials available.) For teens, order the Cash Cache, a thirty-page, beginning personal financial organizer designed to teach teens financial skills, including delayed gratification.

Msmoney.com: The Financial Basics. http://www.msmoney.com /mm/get_started/get_started/index.htm.

SuzyOrman.com: Resource Center. http://www.suzeorman.com.

Tyson, Eric. *Personal Finances for Dummies.* For Dummies Press, 2009.

RAISING CHILDREN

Gallo, Eileen, PhD, and Jon Gallo, JD. *Silver Spoon Kids: How Successful Parents Raise Responsible Children.* Contemporary Books, 2002.

Godfrey, Joline. *Raising Financially Fit Kids: A Parent's Guide to Raising Financially Sophisticated Children.* Ten Speed Press, 2003.

Hausner, Lee, Ph.D. *Children of Paradise: Successful Parenting for Prosperous Families.* Jeremy P. Tarcher, Inc., 1990.

Stovall, Jim. *The Ultimate Gift.* This work of fiction teaches the "gifts" of hard work, family, gratitude, and so on. "What would you do to inherit a million dollars? Would you be willing to change your life? Jason Stevens is about to find out in Jim Stovall's *The Ultimate Gift.* Red Stevens has died, and the older members of his family receive their millions with greedy anticipation. But a different fate awaits young Jason, whom Stevens, his great-uncle, believes may be the last vestige of hope in the family. 'Although to date your life seems to be a sorry excuse for anything I would call promising, there does seem to be a spark of something in you that I hope we can fan into a flame. For that reason, I am not making you an instant millionaire.' What Stevens does give Jason leads to The Ultimate Gift. Young and old will take this timeless tale to heart." (From the publisher's description, www.amazon.com.)

Classic Parenting Resources

Kaye, Kenneth. *Family Rules: Raising Responsible Children.* iUniverse, Inc., 2005. A 1984 publication, updated in 2005, written by respected psychologist and family therapist, Dr. Kenneth Kaye. This practical guide explains how to custom design for your own family a set of straightforward rules that make discipline easy.

Nelsen, Jane, Ed.D. *Positive Discipline.* Rev. ed. Ballantine, 2006. The classic guide is for parents and teachers to help children develop self-discipline, responsibility, cooperation, and problem-solving skills.

Inheritor Issues

Bronfman, Joanie. *The Experience of Inherited Wealth: A Social-Psychological Perspective.* University of Michigan Dissertation Services, 1993.

The Inheritance Project: www.inheritance-project.com. Founded in 1992 to explore the emotional and social impact of inherited wealth. Publications on inheritance can be ordered from the web site.

Johnson, Jamie (dir.). *Born Rich.* 2002. Documentary film by first-time filmmaker Jamie Johnson, a twenty-three-year-old heir to the

Johnson & Johnson pharmaceutical fortune. Johnson captures the rituals, worries, and social customs of the young Trumps, Vanderbilts, Newhouses, and Bloombergs in the documentary special, offering candid insights into the privileges and burdens of inheriting more money than most people will earn in a lifetime.

Levy, John L. *Coping with Inherited Wealth*. Rev. ed. 1999. Available at www.levy842al@aol.com.

O'Neill, Jessie H. *The Golden Ghetto: The Psychology of Affluence*. Hazelden Publications, 1996.

Willis, Thayer Cheatham. *Navigating the Dark Side of Wealth: A Life Guide for Inheritors*. New Concord Press, 2003.

PHILANTHROPY AND CHARITY

Bach, David. *Smart Women Finish Rich*. Broadway Books, 1999.

Brest, Paul, and Hal Harvey. *Money Well Spent: A Strategic Guide to Smart Philanthropy*. Bloomberg Press, 2008. "An invaluable resource that distills the essence of strategic philanthropy for those seeking to achieve a greater social impact." —Bill Gates, Co-Chair, Bill & Melinda Gates Foundation.

Collier, Charles. *Wealth in Families*. Harvard University Press, 2000. Collier's popular book offers a clear, coherent understanding of the role philanthropy can play in helping families convey both values and wealth across the generations.

Gary, Tracy, and Melissa Kohner. *Inspired Philanthropy*. Jossey Bass, 2002. A step-by-step guide to creating a giving plan that shows how to align giving with one's deepest values.

Karoff, Peter. *The World We Want: New Dimensions in Philanthropy and Social Change*. AltaMira Press, 2006.

Raymond, Susan, and Mary Beth Martin. *Mapping the New World of American Philanthropy: Causes and Consequences of the Transfer of Wealth*. Wiley, 2007. Authoritative essays on the impact of wealth transfer on philanthropy.

Remer, Ellen. "When Giving is Gaining: A Strategic Approach to Philanthropy." In *Wealthy and Wise*, ed. Heidi Steiger. Wiley, 2003.

Salamon, Julie. *Rambam's Ladder: A Meditation on Generosity and Why it is Necessary to Give*. Workman Publishing, 2003. Salamon was inspired to write *Rambam's Ladder* by the events of September 11. This very personal book draws on Salamon's lifetime of experience with volunteering and charitable giving. Rambam's "Ladder" (from the twelfth century) is an eight-step continuum of charity, from the lowest form, "Reluctance" (giving begrudgingly) to the highest, "Responsibility," which is to give the gift of self-reliance, as in the adage "teach a man to fish and he will eat for a lifetime."

Stovall, Jim. *The Ultimate Gift.* This work of fiction teaches the "gifts" of hard work, family, gratitude, and so on. "What would you do to inherit a million dollars? Would you be willing to change your life? Jason Stevens is about to find out in Jim Stovall's *The Ultimate Gift.* Red Stevens has died, and the older members of his family receive their millions with greedy anticipation. But a different fate awaits young Jason, whom Stevens, his great-uncle, believes may be the last vestige of hope in the family. 'Although to date your life seems to be a sorry excuse for anything I would call promising, there does seem to be a spark of something in you that I hope we can fan into a flame. For that reason, I am not making you an instant millionaire.' What Stevens does give Jason leads to The Ultimate Gift. Young and old will take this timeless tale to heart." (From the publisher's description, www.amazon.com.)

Social Venture Philanthropy

Social Venture Partners (SVP): www.svpseattle.org. An organization that links community professionals and nonprofit organizations to make a hands-on difference. Established to build a philanthropic organization using a venture capital model, where partners actively nurture their financial investments with guidance and resources. Partners make a minimum charitable donation, research issues, and make investment decisions. They're aided by workshops and other resources to make them more effective community leaders, and most volunteer with nonprofits who receive grants. Available in over twenty-three cities.

Web-Based Philanthropic Resources

American Institute of Philanthropy (AIP): www.charitywatch.org. The AIP is a national charity watchdog service whose purpose is to help donors make informed giving decisions.

Better Business Bureau's Wise Giving Alliance: www.give.org. Information on hundreds of nonprofit organizations that solicit nationally or have national or international program services.

Charity Navigator: www.charitynavigator.org. This organization is a top-tier independent charity evaluator, working to advance a more efficient and responsive philanthropic marketplace by evaluating the financial health of over 5,300 of America's largest charities. Their web site includes numerous "top ten" lists of charities.

Community Foundation Directory: www.communityfoundation locator.org. Resource for community foundations.

Council on Foundations: www.cof.org. The Council on Foundations is a membership organization of more than 2,000 grant-making foundations and giving programs worldwide. COF provides leadership expertise, legal services, and networking opportunities, and provides national support services for different sectors of philanthropy, including family foundations. COF also offers conferences, reference publications, and referrals to regional associations of grant-makers.

The Foundation Center: fdncenter.org. Founded in 1956, dedicated to advancing knowledge about U.S. philanthropy.

Grantmakers without Borders: www.internationaldonors.org. Information and resources for international giving.

National Center for Family Philanthropy (NCFP): www.ncfp.org. NCFP's mission is to promote philanthropic values, vision, and excellence across generations of donors and donor families.

NewTithing Group: www.newthithing.org. This group helps donors determine affordable charitable giving levels. It produces educational tools such as published guides and booklets, a budgeting advisor, web site columns, and news and speaking engagements.

PHILOSOPHY/SPIRITUALITY OF MONEY

Mogil, Chris, and Ann Slepian. *We Gave Away a Fortune.* New Society Publishers, 1991.

Needleman, Jacob. *Money and the Meaning of Life.* Currency/Doubleday, 1991.

Twist, Lynne. *The Soul of Money: Transforming Your Relationship with Money and Life.* W. W. Norton & Company, 2003.

INDEX